Praise for
Inv

"I have been reading Mark's blog postings for a while now, and think he's a straight-shooter - no promises of overnight riches, just tips to use so you can succeed with money and time.

I have three rentals and own my own home. I haven't bought a rental since the real estate fiasco due to the tightened lending restrictions, but want to buy more rentals now. I want to get great deals, and - biggest for me- want to figure out how I can finance them with four mortgages already under my name.

I have learned some great strategies from this program and plan to try them out as soon as possible. One of which is to get my realtor's license so I can see the good deals quickly!" —Nancy

---

"You are amazing, Mark! Thank you for so generously sharing your experience & suggestions for those of us who are uncertain about what to do next.

I have much more confidence about moving forward while "Pre-MF" there were so many questions unanswered I felt immobilized & feared making any moves.

Thank you thank you!!!" -Karen Hanson-Carson

"Hello Mark, I wanted to thank you for advice you'd given about bidding on HUD homes. I followed your advice (being the first one to bid after the owner occupant period ends) and won my first HUD home. It's a great deal here in the Cleveland area and I'll be closing soon. Again, thanks!"-Donald Willis, Cleveland, Ohio

---

"Loving all the stuff you share and teach. Been a long time reader and you continue to amaze and inspire. Thank you for the blog and videos!"

 INVESTFOURMORE

HOW TO CHANGE YOUR MINDSET TO ACHIEVE HUGE SUCCESS

Why your attitude and daily habits have more to do with making more money having more freedom than anything else

MARK FERGUSON

ASIN: B00M8LEZWI

Cover Design: Pixel Studio

Interior Design: Justin Gesso

Editing: Jeremiah Dalton

Printed in the USA

Table of Contents

DEDICATION

Thank you to Jack Canfield Coaching and my personal coach John Beaman, who taught me many of the techniques in this book.

Special Bonus and Investing Tools

This book can be applied to any career or business, but I found most of my success through real estate. If you are interested in learning more about investing in real estate or being a real estate agent, I have some special bonuses for my readers.

I have reached millions of people with my books and blog posts. I receive success stories all the time about how my books, articles, and coaching products have helped people.

I have many free resources on my website, an awesome podcast, and much more.

I written multiple books, created video coaching programs, and created coaching programs with personal help from me.

To learn more about what I have to offer, check out this page and get your special discount code.

https://investfourmore.com/bonus

HOW TO USE THIS BOOK

This book goes through what I have learned about success. I am not a billionaire, I am sure there will be people worth much more than me that read this book. However, I have balanced wealth with family and happiness. I know many people claim you cannot find huge success with a balanced life, but I do not find that true. I am also continuously growing and improving.

I found success with real estate, but I also found myself working 80 hours a well and constantly stressed about money and life. It seemed the more money that I made, the more stress that came with it. I had more bills, more responsibilities, and more to lose! Through coaching programs I went through and by building passive income I basically eliminated that stress and worry. The answer was not making more money, it was looking at life differently, and living in the now. There are also tasks and routines that you can implement to make yourself more successful, happier, and have less stress. This book will help you create a game plan for your life, both professionally and personally.

Below are a few highlights of my career (I am 37 now). I am by no means done, but I am not someone writing about success, who has never seen any.

- I own 16 rentals that make me about $8,000 a month. I bought each rental with 20 or 25 percent down and bought them at least 25 percent market value.
- My 16 rentals have over 1.6 million dollars in equity and I invested about $300,000 to buy and renovate them starting in 2010. That is a pretty decent return.
- I have been a Realtor for 15 years and run a real estate sales team of 10, who sell from 100 to 200 houses a year

- I also flip 10 to 15 houses a year. As of June 2016, I have 10 flips going at once and average about a $30,000 profit on each flip I complete.
- I started InvestFourMore.com in 2013 and it has since become one of the most popular real estate blogs with over 300,000 views a month.
- I have been featured on the Washington Post, MSN, Yahoo, Zilllow, Realtor.com, The Street, Forbes, The Huffington Post and many other large media outlets.

There is a lot of information in this book. There are many techniques, which can become overwhelming. Do not try to do everything at once! If you only learn one thing the first time reading this book, it will help you. The next time you read it, maybe you implement a few other things and slowly start building a solid foundation for success. If you take your time mastering one thing at a time, you will be much more successful than if you halfway do 10 things at once.

It may help to take notes while you read or to pause frequently on the things that really hit home with you, or you feel will help you the most.

If you like this book, please let me know. Mark@investfourmore.com. I personally respond to all emails I get and love hearing from my readers. Please leave me a review on Amazon as well. If you are looking for a little more help or even more details I have additional resources available on my blog at https://investfourmore.com/resources/

INTRODUCTION

When I graduated from college in 2001, I thought I had the world by the horns. I had a degree in business finance, I was smart, and I knew I would be successful. The only problem I had, was I had no plan, no idea what I wanted to do for work, and I wasn't the hardest worker. For some reason, I was not super successful right out of college! I ended up working for my dad part-time in real estate, which became full-time and then an awesome business. I struggled in the beginning of my career, not because I was in the wrong field, or I was not knowledgeable, but because I had a bad attitude and did not know how to be successful.

I thought I was smart, I was educated, I thought I could be successful, but there is much more to success than intelligence and education. Hard work is also a very important part of success, and although I could have definitely worked a little harder in school and at work, that wasn't the missing piece to the puzzle. Not only did I struggle after college, I became very frustrated with where my career was going. I lost some of my dreams, I started to tell myself I didn't want fancy things or nice cars, because I started to believe I would never be able to get those things. If I convinced myself, I didn't want those things, maybe I would be less disappointed.

A funny thing happened a few years into my real estate career. I got fed up with how things were going and I made some drastic changes. At first the changes resulted in me making much less money and being way more stressed! However, I accidently started to create some goals, because I got fed up with how things were going. Then I started to listen to other people and not rely on just myself. I got outside my comfort zone and did things that scared me and were very hard to do. My life started to turn around, and success followed very quickly.

I went from having a goal to make $100,000 a year to a goal to make $1,000,000 a year in a few years. I found success in multiple businesses. I built a team that reduced my stress and time I worked. I became happier, I bought an awesome house, had an awesome family and even bought a Lamborghini (a life-long dream). The more successful I became, the more I realized that success was not about intelligence, hard work or even education. It was about belief, planning, confidence and structure.

In this book I will tell you a little more about my story. How I made $28,000 in 2006, but now have 16 rentals, flip 10 to 15 houses a year, run a real estate team of ten and work less than 40 hours a week. I could retire at the age of 37, but I have big goals and big aspirations, plus I love what I do!

1. HOW TO BE MORE SUCCESSFUL IN LIFE

I have been very successful in real estate, but not because I was lucky or extremely smart. I did not become very successful in real estate until 2008 and 2009, even though I became an agent in 2001. In 2006, I only made $28,000 the entire year! I made so little money, because I made some big mistakes professionally and personally, but I am glad that year happened. That year lit a fire underneath me and forced me to make some big changed.

Being successful in real estate or life is not just about knowledge, hard work, or luck. Many real estate agents and investors have just as much knowledge as I do and work very hard, but have not been successful. I am not trying to brag, but to show there is more to being successful than knowledge and working hard. I follow a plan that involves many different actions and strategies to help be successful. I have many goals and plans, read self-help books, mediate, surround myself with great people, I am constantly trying to improve myself, and I never stop learning.

SHARING MY STRATEGIES FOR SUCCESS IN LIFE

I hear people talk about how goals do not work, how being positive does not work, how doing what you love will never make you money, or that you have to be lucky to be successful. I think Brian Tracy has a great attitude towards luck,

"I've found that luck is quite predictable. If you want more luck, take more chances, be more active, show up more often."

— Brian Tracy

As soon as I started setting goals, making plans according to those goals, and taking action, my luck changed and my life changed for the better. When I started reading self-help books and taking additional steps to improve myself, things got better. So what about the people who have tried to set goals or be positive and it did not work for them? I think there is more to being successful than setting a couple of goals, being happy occasionally, or reading one self-help book. Another great quote from Jim Rohn,

"Work harder on yourself than you do on your job."
— Jim Rohn

I have read many self-help books and listened to many audio CDs telling me how to improve my life. I have also taken Jack Canfield coaching and I am always looking for better ways to improve how I do things. It is not a quick and easy fix to change your attitude and beliefs about being successful. When I took Jack Canfield coaching, I had to spend 10 hours a week on assignments. It takes about three weeks to build a habit. Most people start something new and quit, unless they absolutely have to do it. They get excited for a day or two, then realize what they started was too hard, or there are better things to do with their time. There is not just one thing you can change in a couple of day to become successful, it is a process that takes time, sometimes years.

Being successful is not about setting a couple of goals, it is about creating and following a system that helps get your mind in the right place to be successful. You have to do many things differently to be successful and it takes a lot of work in the beginning. The people who criticize goal setting, probably never spent the time it takes to break down goals into actionable steps. The people who think being positive is worthless, have probably not read books on the reasons it works or coupled being positive with goal setting, taking action, or visualization. They also assumed being positive would not help and big surprise, it didn't! You also have to have belief and faith that what you are doing will work, or you are sabotaging yourself from the very beginning.

SUCCESS IS NOT JUST ABOUT MONEY

My hope is that I can help others achieve success, be more successful than they are already, or just be happier. I am not a certified life coach or a self-help guru, but these techniques have helped me be more successful, happier, and have more free time. When I started making more money, I was not really happier. I was actually stressed out, because I felt I should be doing more with what I had. I was also worried what would happen if I lost my income and everything I had worked so hard for. Success is not just about making more money, but being happier and enjoying that money.

DO NOT STRESS ABOUT CHANGING YOUR LIFE OVERNIGHT

One of the most important things I learned over the last couple of years, is to relax. Do not stress about the past, because you cannot change it. Do not stress about the future, because you do not know what will happen. Do what you can do now to be successful, but it will not happen overnight. I think the more we relax the happier we are. I try to improve every day, but I know I cannot do everything at once. Having twelve flips at one time can be very stressful, and I wish they were all completed and on the market right now, but that is not going to happen. All I can do is keep working hard on the most important things I can in my business, to make it run better. Stressing about what has happened or what might happen will not help my business. Planning for the future, but working hard on the important things, will help things.

A really good book I just read, is the power of now. It talks about how too many people live in the past or the future and forget about today. I find myself constantly thinking how awesome things will be when this happens, or just wait until I get past this hurdle! It is good to plan for the future and imagine how great things will be, but it is also important to appreciate the present and how awesome things are now. We all have many things to be thankful for, even if it doesn't seem like it on certain days.

CONCLUSION

The first step in changing your life, and being more successful is to not stress about doing everything. There are a lot of techniques and tips in this book. By implementing one at a time, you can be happier and more successful. You do not have to do everything at once and do not feel bad if it takes time to create habits and change. Most people never take the time to consciously think about their life, their success and their happiness. Most float through life, so you are already ahead of the curve.

2. YOU MUST MAKE YOUR OWN SUCCESS, IT WILL NOT HAPPEN FOR YOU

Many people complain that life is not fair, and they cannot succeed because of circumstances beyond their control. It is true that life can throw us curve balls, but successful people do not let those curve balls distract them. The truth is, most successful and unsuccessful people have the same amount of luck and opportunities. The successful people, take advantage of the opportunities they are given or they make their own opportunities. For a long time I waited for success to come to me in the real estate business and it never came. I decided it would not just come to me; I had to go out and get it!

A great saying I recently heard was:

"If you are born poor it is not your mistake, but if you die poor it is your mistake."

— Bill Gates

OUR NATURAL TENDENCY IS TO SIT BACK AND NOT TAKE CHANCES

It is easy to say you will go out and get success, but it is not easy to do it. For most of us, the natural thing to do is to sit back, stay on the same track, and hope the future will bring us what we are looking for. The hard thing, is to change our track, do something different, take chances, and get out of our comfort zone. If your boss does not see your value, if your investments are not doing well, if you cannot save money, change something. These issues do not magically fix themselves; you have to fix them by changing your attitude, habits, and actions.

I had done traditional real estate since 2001 with limited success. In 2008 and 2009, I began to see a lot of success after I started listing REO properties. I knew something had to change if I wanted to achieve everything I wanted out of life. I went out on a limb and started pursuing REO listings with a passion. I was very shy as a child and I still am a bit of an introvert. However, I picked up the phone and started cold calling banks to see how I could list their foreclosures. I hated the phone at the time, and it was not easy for me to call people I had never talked to (probably why I was not a successful traditional real estate agent). I did not even know if the banks would have any idea what I was talking about when I asked about listing REO properties. Those calls got me the information I needed to get my foot in the door with banks.

After that, I went to conferences by myself not knowing anyone there. I was nervous as ****, but I did it anyway. I made friends, I talked to people and it was one of the best things I ever did. Since then, I have spoken at conferences in front of hundreds of people. I still do not like talking on the phone and I am still an introvert, but that did not stop me. Being an introvert was not stopping me from talking to people or taking chances, my own fear was stopping me, being an introvert was just an excuse.

ONCE YOU FIND SOME SUCCESS YOU CANNOT SIT BACK AND RELAX

Once you find a little success, you cannot sit back and enjoy the ride. I have learned that it is much more fun to keep changing things up and pursuing new ideas, than to be "comfortable". Once I started listing REO properties, I began joining REO groups such as the NRBA. I attended the NRBA conference, which was way out of my comfort zone. I found myself in a group of REO brokers who had listed bank owned properties for ten times longer than I had, and were making five times the money I was. I was in awe and did not think I belonged with that group of successful people. When I talked to them, did they look down on me and wonder what I was doing with them? Did they ignore me and turn their back on me, because I was not as successful? No. They spent more time with me, because they knew they could help me more than others there. They did not make fun of me for not making as much money, they kept telling me to wait until I made that much and how awesome it would be. They assumed I would make it big, even if I did not. Today I sell as many houses as they do, plus I have three more business that bring in healthy incomes.

After I began making as much money as the REO brokers I was previously in awe of, I did not sit back and relax. I looked for more ways to improve my business and life. I researched the best ways to invest my money, started reading self-help books, and enrolled in personal coaching. Thanks to personal coaching, I was convinced to take more chances and be willing to move even farther out of my comfort zone. I started *Invest Four More*, took over the real estate and fix-and-flip business from my father, and continued to grow. I learned how to delegate more, gain more free time, and relax. In the beginning of 2013, I even volunteered to speak in front of 200 people at a conference. With my previous attitude, I would have never volunteered to speak in front of more than five people (or anyone at all). I am extremely proud of that amazing experience. All this happened because I was willing to try new things, that I had no idea would work out. Ten years ago, I would have laughed at the idea of doing any of this. I would have assumed there is no way I could ever do those things.

It is a good thing I did not relax. If I had relaxed after doing well in REO, I would be in trouble now because there is currently so little REO in our area. Luckily, I did not sit back, I created new streams of income and continued to grow.

WHEN CAN YOU GET COMFORTABLE?

Many people have a goal of making enough money "to be comfortable in life". The idea of being comfortable seems appealing; sit back, relax, and all your problems will be gone. However, if you look at the most successful people, they do not ever get comfortable. They keep trying new things, taking chances, and moving out of their comfort zone.

Why would people continue to go outside their comfort zone? Because it is exciting and fun to continue to try new things and take chances. When you start thinking of problems as challenges, life becomes much more fun. When you stop worrying about problems and simply start doing the best you can with what you have, life is much more fun. Life is not about being comfortable, it is about getting the most you can out of life while conquering challenges. Real estate has provided me with a great income and investments. People see what I have done and wonder how they will ever get there. I see what I have done, and wonder how I can reach the people I look up to. How can I reach the next level and the next level after that? Is it stressful for me to constantly be striving for more? Not if I remember to live in the present and be thankful for what I have now. I enjoy life thoroughly, even though I want to keep going and improving. Every time I do something new, it is fun for me. I learn more, I get excited, and I am passionate. When I accomplish success in something new, it is an awesome feeling and way better than being "comfortable".

For those that have a goal of making a ton of money and then retiring to the beach. Awesome! Retiring to the beach is a specific goal and will be exciting and different than what you are doing now. I do not call retiring to the beach as being comfortable. Being comfortable is sitting at home, where you live now, with enough money that you don't really have to worry about bills and you can probably retire at a decent age. That is another problem with "being comfortable", the term is not well defined for most people. Most people who say they want to be comfortable, have not defined exactly what that means to them. To some it may mean not being late on bills, to others, it may mean retiring on the beach!

CONCLUSION

Your state of mind is one of the most important attributes for success. You have to be willing to change, take chances, and make things happen. Ninety percent of the ultra-wealthy became wealthy on their own without an inheritance or winning the lottery. Wealth and happiness did not come to them; they went out and got it. If you are not happy with how things are going, do something different, take chances, and educate yourself. Do not stress about getting over the hump and someday being comfortable; live your life now and embrace change and excitement.

3. Is the world a good environment to succeed in?

Every time I read or watch the news, there seems to be a story about the world falling apart. Terrorism is everywhere, our children aren't safe walking alone, crime is increasing and our economy is on shaky ground. If you go on Facebook it can be even worse with anti-gun, pro-gun, anti-Obama, anti-Trump, anti-Hillary, anti-global warming, pro-global warming and it goes on and on. We are constantly bombarded with terrifying news and how our world is going to end, if things aren't changed soon. Many feel these topics are important if you are investing in real estate, because these events affect the economy and housing prices. While some of the news may be important, I think if you get too wrapped up in how bad everything is, it will make it hard to be successful. I was a little worried about writing this chapter, because I did not want to push away readers based on my political views. Hopefully after reading this you will see it is not about my views, but about success and how paying too much attention to the negatives can greatly hurt your chances of succeeding. I also think the world is in a much better place than the news makes it out to be.

Is the world really as bad off as the news suggests?

Just about every day there is news of people being killed, mass shootings, terrorism and economies falling apart. Yes, there are shootings and deaths every day, but there are also 7 billion people in the world and over 300 million people in the United States. When you have that many people in the world, bad things are going to happen. There will be accidents, there will be wars, there will be famine and there will be negative things happening all the time. If you know me at all, you know that I am a numbers guy. When I see stories in the news or posts on Facebook about one story, which proves the world is falling apart, or proves a political viewpoint one way or the other, it drives me crazy.

I am not going to get into my personal views, but when you analyze a situation that involves billions of people, you have to look at massive studies or historical figures to see what is really happening. One story about one person out of 300 million, does not prove a trend or a point. With billions of people in the world, it is guaranteed that you could find a story that would prove any point you want to prove. When you ask what do the numbers say? You start to see what is really going on.

- Children are much safer today than at any point in our history. http://www.businessinsider.com/american-children-safer-than-ever-2015-4. Do abductions and bad things happen? Yes, but they are happening much less now than they ever did. So all those stories about it being so much safer to walk to school when your parents were kids, are just not true. Children are much safer today than ever before in almost all aspects: car accidents, diseases, crime, etc.
- Terrorism deaths of US citizens is minuscule compared to many other causes of death. Here is a great chart on the deaths caused by terrorism in the US. Note there were 32 fatalities world-wide in 2014 (more lately, but still relatively few), which is much less than what was occurring in the late 1990's. Here are the leading causes of death in the United States:
  - Heart disease: 611,105
  - Cancer: 584,881
  - Chronic lower respiratory diseases: 149,205

- Accidents (unintentional injuries): 130,557
- Stroke (cerebrovascular diseases): 128,978
- Alzheimer's disease: 84,767
- Diabetes: 75,578
- Influenza and Pneumonia: 56,979
- Nephritis, nephrotic syndrome, and nephrosis: 47,112
- Intentional self-harm (suicide): 41,149

- <u>The world overall is safer than it ever has been according to many reports.</u>

While many people feel terrorism is their biggest concern, a 15 to 24-year-old is much more likely to die from a heart attack, cancer and many other diseases, than a terrorist. Over 30,000 people die in car accidents every year. But, the news and politicians scare us into thinking we are all in danger of being shot by terrorists. It is possible we could be killed in an attack, but when you look at the numbers, there are much more dangerous things that we should be much more worried about.

I saw a Facebook post from someone who was cancelling their trip to Europe, because of recent terrorist attacks. I could not believe how many people agreed that we should not travel to Europe because of terrorists. The chances of dying in a car accident in the United States 1,000 times greater than being killed by a terrorist in Europe. That means it may actually be safer to travel to Europe, if you are not driving there, than it is to stay here and drive to work every day.

While the news makes it appear the world is falling apart, we actually live in a very safe era. You also live in an era with tons of opportunity, if you are able to ignore all the negatives out there.

HOW CAN ALL THIS NEGATIVITY HURT YOUR CHANCES OF SUCCESS?

To be honest, I used to get caught up in political arguments and the negativity that the news pumps out every day. I don't think people realize how much time they spend arguing politics, especially if they actually research the issues. When you try to research politics with actual numbers and unbiased opinions, it can take hours to find one decent source! I would spend so much time arguing with people on Facebook or in person, that it actually hurt my business. In fact conducting research for this article has taken a ton of time and is frustrating me as well, because it is so hard to find decent information. If you are constantly arguing with people, what are you sacrificing? How could you use that time better to educate yourself or make your business better?

The other issue that poses a problem with politics and the negativity in the world, is what it does to your mindset. I am a huge believer that the more positive and happy someone is, the more successful they will be. The happier you are, the better you work, the more opportunities you see and the more people will want to work with you. If you are always pissed off or worried, it will make it much harder to be successful in life.

If you take the news or some politicians as the truth, it could also hurt your real estate investing. If all you did was listen to the news, it would seem that every market in the United States was dangerous and the economy could collapse at any moment. If you are buying rentals or flips, this could affect your business. I am not saying you should not look at the economy or crime rate when you invest in an area, but look at the statistics, don't believe the news.

Just because housing prices are increasing, it does not mean housing prices will crash again. I hear investors tell me they aren't buying until the next housing crash, but they may never buy if they wait for a crash like we had before. When the news warns that the economy is horrible and the high housing prices mean a crash is coming. Should you listen to the media who are trying to scare people constantly and have no clue what will happen, or should you do the research yourself and come up with your own conclusions?

WHAT IF YOU FEEL A MORAL OBLIGATION TO INFORM OTHERS THE DANGERS OF THE WORLD?

There are some that feel they need to be an advocate and tell others the truths about the world and why things need to change. Whether telling the world why things need to change will help anything or not, think about this:

"Entrepreneurs are needed to create and grow companies to absorb those people in new jobs. If entrepreneurs don't create those jobs, the government ends up having to spend more money to help them one way or another.

So be patriotic. Go out there and get rich. Get so obnoxiously rich that when that tax bill comes, your first thought will be to choke on how big a check you have to write. Your second thought will be "what a great problem to have", and your third should be a recognition that in paying your taxes you are helping to support millions of Americans that are not as fortunate as you."

-Mark Cuban

Instead of complaining about taxes, arguing about politics or worrying about how dangerous the world is. Take that energy and improve yourself, educate yourself and become more successful. The best way to change the world, is to be the best person you can be, hire people, make a ton of money, pay a lot of taxes and improve the economy, and lives of people closest to you.

HOW DO YOU MAKE YOURSELF STOP WORRYING ABOUT POLITICS AND THE WORLD?

If you have been arguing politics for a long time, it can be a hard habit to break. If you have been hesitant to invest or start a business because the world is falling apart, it can be hard to get over that fear. There are simple things that will help you stop worrying about things you cannot change and start focusing on things you can change.

- Don't reply or post anything political on Facebook. This invites arguments and one person who disagrees with you, can eat up hours of time you could have used for much more productive things.
- If people are filling up your news feed with constant negativity and junk, delete them. It is easy to do and if you hurt their feelings too bad. They are probably used to people deleting them anyway. (It's not the worst thing in the world to stay away from social media in general, unless it is my Facebook page)
- If you don't think the world is safe, or the economy is in good shape, do some research! Don't blindly follow the news without checking out the statistics for yourself. Ask other business people in your area, ask other successful people what their thoughts are.
- Make sure you surround yourself with the right people. If you are always around negative people, it is really hard to be positive yourself. Even if you are positive, you probably think negative thoughts about the person

wishing they weren't so negative! Listen to the people who are the most successful. You will start to see the successful people are the most positive, while the negative people don't have much going on.

CONCLUSION

There will always be conflict, terrorism and bad people. You cannot change that and you cannot constantly worry that something will happen to you. The world is safer now, more than it ever has been. Most people are spending too much time worrying about dangers that have almost no chance of occurring and ignoring dangers that could affect them greatly. To make a difference and change the world, spend your time and energy on becoming an overwhelming success. You will be happier, you will help more people and make a difference in the world.

4. To Succeed in Life You Must Live in the Present; No Regrets, No Worrying

One of the greatest lessons I learned in personal coaching, was to stop worrying about the past and the future. The past has already happened and having regrets will not change it. However, you can learn from the past and treat past mistakes as opportunities to learn. We do not know what will happen in the future, but many of us expect the worst and worry constantly. We can prepare as best we are able for the future, but we cannot predict the future and it does no good worrying about bad things that may happen.

- I usually have over ten fix and flips going at a time. Many times, it takes me way too long to sell my flips and I wish I would have sold them weeks or months ago. I cannot change the fact I have held on to some properties too long. All I can do, is my best to get them ready to sell to make the most money I can.
- I did not start taking my real estate career seriously until I had been in the business seven years. I cannot kick myself for waiting so long, but I can learn from those mistakes.
- Interest rates may rise in the future making it hard to buy more rentals, or hurt the real estate market. However, I do not know for sure if interest rates will rise and if they do, I do not know that it will hurt my investing. I will not ignore the fact that rates could rise, but I am not going to worry about it either, because I cannot change them anyway.

THE BOOK THAT HELPED ME RELAX MORE THAN ANYTHING

My coach from jack Canfield coaching, told me some of his students think one book: *Too Perfect: When Being in Control Gets out of Control*, by Jeannette Dewyze, was worth the entire coaching fee. This book is all about obsessive-compulsive behavior. When I first saw what this book was about, I thought that I was the farthest thing from obsessive-compulsive! I learned to keep an open mind about things and I read the book thinking I could learn at least one thing that would help me improve my life. I learned about 1,000 things that would help me improve my life and I learned I was actually very obsessive-compulsive. Obsessive-compulsive behavior is not reserved for clean freaks or those with obvious compulsive tendencies. I would guess that most successful people are very obsessive-compulsive, but do not realize it or realize how much it is hindering their lives and success.

Obsessive-compulsive tendencies include many characteristics that most people would consider habits of a successful person. Some of those traits the book describes include:

- Getting caught up in details when completing tasks
- Making sure work projects are perfect, no matter how long it takes
- Having trouble making decisions
- Second guessing yourself make after you make a decision
- Refusing to show emotion, because you are worried what others will think
- Being worried that people are always trying to rip you off
- Always trying to get the best deal, no matter how much time to takes
- Wanting to do everything yourself, because you do not trust others to do the job right
- Constantly thinking about work or other problems, even when you are not working and are supposed to be relaxing
- Constantly considering what could go wrong when thinking about future events
- Getting extremely upset when people are critical of your work or unhappy with you, even when the criticism is justified

- Feeling guilty when you are not doing something productive even during your time off

As you can see, many of these traits are things that very successful and driven people do all the time!

WHY IS IT BAD TO BE OBSESSIVE-COMPULSIVE IN LIFE AND WORK?

I can say from personal experience that I had many obsessive-compulsive traits. I constantly worried about the future and money, even when I was making good money. I would wonder what would happen if I lost my income or if all of my business went away. Have I saved enough money or invested enough? These are good things to think about, but they should not dominate your thoughts all the time. I would get anxious and actually feel sick sometimes when thinking about money and the future. After reading the book, *Too Perfect*, I was able to relax about so many things, mostly because I realized it did no good to worry. The book not only helps you realize where you might be obsessive-compulsive in your life, but also helps you figure out how to fix those tendencies.

Part of being successful in life and business is having time to plan your future, relax with your family, and be happy. If you are constantly worrying about the future, worrying about work, and dwelling on the past, you are not enjoying life. You will not have free time to plan for the future and make your life better. If you can learn to relax, stop worrying about things you cannot control or change, and live in the present, your life will improve dramatically.

HOW CAN YOU STOP WORRYING AND FREE UP MORE TIME COMPLETING TASKS?

Too Perfect goes into detail on how to improve your life and let go. It helped me tremendously by allowing me to live in the now and stop worrying. One great tip in the book was most tasks do not need to be perfect. In work, it may take two hours to complete a task ninety percent of the way, but the next ten percent to make it perfect, may take another two hours. Getting a task perfect takes a lot of time, and most of the time it does not need to be perfect. Some tasks are extremely important and need to be perfect, but most tasks can be done 90 or 95 percent and still get the job done. Most people will not even know the task was not completed 100 percent except you. It was hard for me to start doing this, especially with REO work that had taken me so long to get. I wanted everything perfect and I was scared to let any of my staff do tasks that were somewhat important. I slowly started allowing myself more wiggle room and allowing my staff to complete more important tasks. A funny thing happened, my work improved!

My staff was perfectly capable of completing these tasks and in some cases, they were better than I was. The problem was, I was trying to complete 100 different things at once and my work suffered because of it. I was also slower at getting tasks done, because I wanted them perfect and I wanted to do them all myself. When I delegated and realized every task did not have to be perfect, I got more done and it was done faster, which is sometimes more important than things being done perfectly.

HOW CAN YOU RELAX MORE BY FORGETTING THE PAST AND NOT WORRYING ABOUT THE FUTURE?

Another key component of my coaching and the book, *Too Perfect*, was forgetting about the past. Many of us dwell on mistakes we have made or have regrets about how we handled things in the past. The truth is we cannot change the past, no matter how hard we try. It does no good to have regrets or worry about how dumb we were a couple of years ago, when we missed that opportunity. Yes, we can learn from the past; everything we have done in our lives educates us and helps make us who we are today. When I started thinking of the past as education and not stupid mistakes, I felt a great sense of relief. For all I know that huge mistake I made was actually a good thing. What we see as mistakes may have been blessings in disguise; maybe that huge opportunity we missed would have not been a great fit for us, even though it worked out for others.

The same holds true for the future; we cannot worry about what has not happened yet. Many people tend to assume the worst will happen when they plan an event, think about money, or anything in the future. The truth is, the worst rarely happens and usually things turn out okay or even great. I like to plan for the worst, but hope for the best. I do not want to be oblivious to dangers that may occur in the future, but I also will not dwell on them. I like to plan for what could go wrong, but concentrate on what could go right, and how awesome it will be once everything goes exactly as planned.

DO NOT WORRY ABOUT WHAT OTHERS THINK OF YOU

I learned a great saying from Jack Canfield. When you are 18, you worry about what others think of you, when you are 40 you stop giving a hoot (insert your own fun word here) what others think of you, and when you are 60, you realize no one was thinking of you at all. Most people are not thinking about you and being critical of your choices. People are worried about themselves and when they are thinking of you, they are thinking about what you think about them. Live your life and do not let what others may think of you, change the way you act and what you love to do. Some people are critical of me for buying a Lamborghini and I completely understand that, but the car makes me happy. Not everyone will agree with my choice and the truth is most people are more worried about their own lives than what I am doing. I am not going to sacrifice my happiness for what I perceive others are thinking about me, especially after I realize most people are thinking about themselves. The majority of people have extremely positive reactions to the car and the car has made me a lot of money through networking or marketing (not to mention doubling in value). It is still easy to let that one person who says you are a jerk for owning a Lamborghini, get to you. Even though there may be 100 other people praising you. **Do not let the naysayers deter you from success or happiness**.

This idea really came into play, when I spoke in front of a couple hundred people at a conference. I was never an outgoing person and I never volunteered to speak in front of anyone. After changing my attitude about life and realizing getting out of my comfort zone was a good thing, I volunteered to speak. It was one of the best things I ever did, and I felt awesome afterwards. People could tell I was not a polished public speaker, but I think they identified with me better because of it. They went out of their way to tell me I did a good job and had great information. When you hear a person speaking, you do not notice their mistakes or miscues, unless they point them out themselves or are super self-conscious about it. Most people watching a person speak in public are thinking: Thank god that is not me up there! It is a cool feeling knowing you have what it takes to risk looking like a fool in order to help give information to others. It is also cool knowing, that other people will never take that risk and you have accomplished something, by doing it.

CONCLUSION

Relaxing and living in the present is one of the most important things you can do to improve your life. It frees up time, makes you happier, and will make you more successful along the way. Do not worry about the past, the future, or what others think; live your own life.

5. WILL PASSIVE INCOME HELP REDUCE STRESS IN YOUR LIFE?

The number one stress in America is money and it has been for years. That stress comes from knowing you could lose your income or it could be reduced greatly. That is because most people count on income from jobs and not passive income that comes in whether you work or not. People worry about if they have enough money to pay the bills, if they are saving enough, if they will have enough in the future, and what would happen if they lost their jobs. There are many things associated with money that cause stress. I was stressed about money in college, as a young adult, and even a couple of years ago when was making well above the average income. Even though it seems like making more money will relive money stress, it does not always work.

I have been very lucky in life to make a decent living, and now I have removed most of the stress I feel related to money. Not because I am making more, but because I am saving more, investing more and I have a different attitude about money. Real estate has been an incredible vehicle to get me to this point, because of the passive income it can provide.

WHY IS MONEY SO STRESSFUL?

Money is stressful, because our lives revolve around it. Our housing, food, transportation, education, jobs and families all revolve around money. For most people the more money you make, the more money you spend, and the more responsibilities you have. Making more money does not always equal less stress, if you have more obligations and more bills to pay. If you have a lot of bills to pay and you lose your job, or have a drop in income, you are in a worse situation than if you made less and had fewer bills. That assumes you did not save or invest, which most Americans do not (76 percent of Americans live paycheck to paycheck).

WHY CAN MAKING MORE MONEY BE MORE STRESSFUL THAN MAKING LESS MONEY?

I already discussed how people who make more money, tend to have more bills and more responsibilities, which creates more stress. But there was another bigger reason that I felt stress and anxiety when I started making decent money. When I started doing very well as a HUD and REO listing agent, I was not buying rentals or investing much money except for a few thousand a year in an IRA.

The stress I felt, came from a feeling that I was wasting the money I was making and I had nothing to show for it. Sure I had a nice house and nice cars, but cars and one personal house are not going to provide much security. I wanted to buy rental properties, but they were expensive, it was hard saving up for a down payment, and an emergency fund if something went wrong.

Something changed a few years ago that really helped reduce my stress level.

WHAT IS PASSIVE INCOME AND HOW CAN IT REDUCE STRESS?

Most people rely on their jobs to make money, and they get paid for the amount of time they put in. The less they work the less money they make. Passive income is money that comes in whether you work or not. It can come from stock dividends, rental properties, businesses, bonds, notes and many other sources. The nice thing about passive income is it keeps coming in, whether you work or not.

I choose to invest in rental properties to give me passive income. Technically rental properties are not completely passive, because you have to do some work to buy them, maintain them and rent them. I use a property manager to reduce much of the work. When you build up enough passive income, you stop worrying about the income you make from your job, because you know you have a cushion if something goes wrong. Maybe that cushion won't cover everything, but it certainly helps.

DID BUYING A RENTAL PROPERTY REDUCE MY STRESS LEVEL?

In December of 2010 I bought my first rental property for just under $100,000. It needed almost no work, and I figured it would rent for around $1,000 a month. At the time I knew a little about rental properties, but not nearly as much as I know now. The property has been a great investment, even though the rent to value ratio was not quite as high as I like to see now.

Did buying one rental property magically reduce my stress level? No, in fact my stress may have been higher after I bought it, because I started second guessing myself on whether I had enough money to buy a rental, if it was a good deal, if I could manage it, etc.

After I had owned the property a few months and it was rented, I felt pretty good about myself. I knew I had a long way to go and buying one property would not meet my goals, but it was a start. I also knew I had invested money in a real asset and I was not wasting it.

DID BUYING MORE RENTAL PROPERTIES AND INCREASING MY PASSIVE INCOME ELIMINATE MONEY STRESS?

Over the years, I bought more and more rental properties. The more properties I bought, the more my passive income increased, and the better I felt about my financial situation. I still felt stress at times and anxiety wondering if I was saving enough and investing enough. I own 16 rental properties now. With each property I buy, my future becomes more secure.

I have about $9,000 a month in passive income coming in from my rental properties at this point. That is a lot of money for most people, and more than the average salary is in America. As I mentioned before, the more money you make, the more you tend to spend. I am not immune to spending more either, although I try to spend much less than I make. I bought a Lamborghini, which was not exactly cheap. That was a huge decision for me and one I did not take lightly. However, I felt really good about buying the car and it did not cause much stress in my life, instead it caused excitement. Part of the reason I was not too stressed, was because I had a lot of passive income coming in from my rentals and other investments as well.

Having passive income coming in every month, did not reduce my stress level about money completely, but it certainly helped a lot. I knew I was investing, building something and not wasting my money. There was something else I did in the last couple of years that reduced my stress level even more.

HOW CAN YOUR ATTITUDE REDUCE YOU STRESS LEVEL ABOUT MONEY?

A couple of years ago I had a good amount of passive income coming in, a great income, a great family and I still stressed about money. I worried about the economy, about my sources of income and if I was doing enough.

I realized that many of the richest people in the world had made fortunes, lost them and made even more money. It wasn't about how much money or stuff you have, it was about what is inside your head. I have learned how to run businesses, how to write a blog, how to buy houses, and many other things. If I happened to lose it all tomorrow, I could make it back again and be just fine.

Realizing that losing everything, would not be that bad reduced stress in my life more than anything. I certainly am not planning on risking everything I have worked for and I do not think I need to. The attitude change and the passive income coupled with each other, have virtually eliminated money stress in my life. I am still striving to do better and be more successful, but now it is all fun instead of worry.

CONCLUSION

Stress is one of the worst things you can put your body and mind through. Stress causes disease and you can't think clearly when you are constantly worried. Passive income will greatly reduce your stress level when it comes to money, but you don't have to have passive income to reduce stress. A simple attitude adjustment towards your beliefs about money can do amazing things. The happier you are and the less stress in your life, the more successful you will be as well.

6. WHY GETTING OUT OF YOUR COMFORT ZONE IS A GOOD THING

We all like to stay in our comfort zone. We get used to things, we form habits, we know what we like and the natural thing to do is keep things working as smooth as possible. In fact, many of us have a goal or ultimate destination to make enough money to "be comfortable". Is living comfortably a goal anyone should have? Is it fun or rewarding to live comfortable all the time? Some of us think it will be fun to be comfortable all the time and not have to worry about anything. But if you look back at your life and the most memorable moments, did they happen when you were comfortable? I highly doubt it, and I highly doubt being comfortable all the time would be fun for most of us. Instead of striving to be comfortable, look for ways to be uncomfortable.

IS IT CRAZY TO WANT TO BE UNCOMFORTABLE?

Most people do not like to be uncomfortable. They do not like to try new things, go to new places or take chances. The main reason for this, is we don't know what will happen when we get out of our comfort zone. If we have done something 100 times, we have a pretty good idea what will happen the next time we do it. It doesn't matter if you are a professional football player, an accountant, a real estate investor, a public speaker, a teacher or engineer. If you have experience doing something and completing tasks, you have an idea of how things will go, when you have to complete those tasks again. If you have been an engineer your entire life, but want to start investing, it can be very intimidating because you have never done it. Even though engineers have a huge advantage when investing because of their background with numbers. Look at dancing with the starts and how professional athletes who are amazing in their perspective sports look like they have two left feet on the dance floor! At least they do when they start, but many of them practice like crazy and learn to dance.

It is not just the professional athletes that end up being good dancers, most of the contestants on dancing shows become decent, if not great dancers. They were able to become good at something that was completely out of their comfort zone because they were willing to practice and try. It is probably one of the most fun experiences for the people to be on shows like that, where they start out horrible and progress to presentable or even great. We can't all be on dancing with the stars, but we can all definitely do things that take us out of our comfort zone. Most of us are able to get out of our comfort zone without the entire world watching us do it on TV! Being uncomfortable may make us nervous, uneasy and fear for the worst, but it also can be exhilarating, fun and make us more successful.

WHAT THINGS DO I REMEMBER THE MOST AND HAVE BEEN THE MOST FUN?

When I look back at my life the things I remember the most and were the most fun were the scariest. When I was safe in my comfort zone I don't remember much of anything. When I really succeeded at work and made huge breakthroughs it was not while I was in my comfort zone waiting for something to happen. Here's a list of some of the things I am willing to share publicly.

Buying cars out-of-state: Since I was in high school I have looked for great deals on cars. I bought a corvette, multiple Toyota Supra's, a Porsche 928, an Audi S4 and a Lamborghini Diablo, from different states (Florida, Oregon, Oklahoma, New York, Washington, California). I bought the Diablo and Audi without ever seeing the cars in person. I bought those cars in different locations, because I saved money and was able to find the cars I wanted. It was an awesome experience traveling to see the cars, and in some cases driving them across the country or seeing them show up in a truck for the first time.

- **Having twins**: I don't know how many guys ever admit they are ready to have kids, but at some point you have to go for it. Having twins was scary and I had no clue what it would be like. Having kids has been awesome and worth the sleepless nights, screaming, fighting and added responsibilities. I think almost anyone who has kids will tell you they are the best thing they ever did with their life. It is definitely not easy to have kids and will take you way out of your comfort zone!

- **Getting married**: I remember my wedding well, but I was not looking forward to a giant party, getting dressed up, standing up in front of hundreds of people and trying to talk to hold meaningful conversation with long-lost relatives. Even though I was way out of my comfort zone, the wedding was a blast! We even took dance lessons and had our first dance to "Fly me to the Moon". The DJ played a different version than we had practiced to for months, but no one noticed we were frazzled and way off the beat.

- **Taking over my father's business:** When I took Jack Canfield coaching, my coach made look at changes that would make the biggest difference in my life. I knew one of those changes was taking over the business from my dad. At the time, I thought to myself it would be impossible to take over the business. There is too much work with payroll, management, expenses and we would have to come up with a price I would pay. I had no idea if my dad even wanted to sell. In the end I started looking at the process and what it would take. I talked to my dad and he said he had been waiting for me to ask him to take over. It went fairly smooth after the lawyers and accountants stopped arguing about how to structure things. It was one of the best decisions I have made business wise. It can be scary being the only one in charge and taking full responsibility, but also very rewarding and it makes it much easier to do business.

- **Buying rentals:** I wanted to buy rental properties for years before I finally pulled the trigger. Things kept coming up like getting married, moving to a new house and real estate income can be very up and down. When I bought my first rental my wife was pregnant with twins. That was a little stressful, but it worked out great and I wish I would have started much sooner.

- **Buying a 500,000 flip:** I am pretty successful, but that does not mean I sit back and relax. I am in the process of buying a flip for $500,000 at the time of writing this book. For some people it is not a big deal, because they deal in that price range all the time. I usually buy my flips for less than $150,000, so it is a big deal for me. It is scary buying a flip for this much money, but also exciting and new.

- **Writing a blog:** I had not written anything since college when I decided to start a blog. I published articles that were full of typos and written horribly (I am slightly better now). People still liked what I had to write and it was really cool getting emails from people saying how I had helped them.

- **Starting a podcast:** I started a podcast this year, which was tough for me. I am not a super out going person and I was nervous doing podcasts for other shows, where all I had to do was answer a few questions. Doing my own podcast, where I had to ask the questions and direct the show was a bigger jump. But it has been a ton of fun and I have met some really awesome guests.

- **Doing live webinars:** I have started doing live webinars which is also out of my comfort zone. Imagine talking about a certain subject for almost an hour with no interaction. I hope people stuck around and liked what I was talking about, but really I don't know until I am done. My first webinar was a huge success and most people did stick around!

- **Calling people:** I have always tried to avoid the phone as much as possible. I try to communicate via email, but that is not always possible. I talk more and more on the phone, but I still have to be careful about the phone sucking my time. This takes me out of my comfort zone for sure, but it also is rewarding. I am realizing the phone can be a great tool and it is fun to talk to people as well. It also improves my business and coaching.

- **Going to conferences:** I went to my first real estate conference by myself with no clue what to expect. It was awesome. I learned a ton and made many friends. I probably would not have met nearly as many people if I had went with someone and was not forced to meet new people.
- **Going to Australia and Europe:** After college and a few years later, I took trips to Europe and Australia. I went by myself and they were both awesome experiences.
- **Speaking at a conference:** I spoke at a REO conference a couple of years ago. It was way out of my comfort zone. I used to dread the teacher calling on me in class, so imagine how I felt about public speaking. I decided I had to get over my fears and I spoke on a panel with four other people in front of about 300 people. It was nerve racking, but I felt awesome after I was done.

WHY GETTING OUT OF YOUR COMFORT ZONE HELPS YOU BE HAPPIER

Doing all of these things were not easy. I second guessed myself before I did them and in some cases they did not work out perfectly. However, in almost all cases I felt good having done something that I was scared to do. How often do we regret doing something that we were scared of (as long as it was not something completely stupid that someone dared you to do)? Usually we regret the things we didn't do, because we were scared, worried about what others would think, or didn't want to take the time to learn.

The things most worth doing in life do not come easily to us.

WHY GETTING OUT OF YOUR COMFORT ZONE MAKES YOU MORE SUCCESSFUL

Not only does getting out of your comfort zone make you happier, feel more accomplished, give you more memories, but it makes you more successful as well. Most people work for someone else, they want a steady paycheck and a secure job. The most successful people start their own business, they take chances, and they do not rely on others for their success. I think people should also realize working for someone else is not always secure. Someone else decides if you should keep your job, not you. When you work for yourself you can't be fired.

Some of the things that have made me successful were very hard to do. I already mentioned taking over the business from my father. Here are a few others:

- **Hiring people:** I have 10 people on my team and it is tough deciding to take on that many people. While it costs money to hire that many people, they make my life much easier and make me more money than if I was doing this on my own.
- **Buying houses with no inspection:** I buy almost every house without an inspection clause now. It is risky, but I know houses so well that I can see most problems without an inspection. I also can get a much better deal by removing the inspection contingency.
- **Buying a lot of flips:** I have 11 flips right now! It is tough to have that many going at once, but I hired a project manager to help me speed up my repair times. I have since fired that project manager and I am using my current team to manage the flips. Being out of your comfort zone is not always easy!

- **Buying 100 rentals:** Creating a goal to buy 100 rentals was out of my comfort zone. Writing about it for thousands of people to see was even more of a challenge. But that goals has made me buy more properties, learn more and be more successful.

CONCLUSION

Most people will stay in their comfort zone, unless they are absolutely forced to get out. If you look back at your life and what you remember the most, and had the most fun doing, it probably happened when you were challenged and doing something you weren't used to. When you make it a point to do things that are different, new and challenging, life becomes a lot more fun. Do you really just want to be "comfortable in life"?

7. WHY BEING POSITIVE WILL HELP YOU BECOME MORE SUCCESSFUL

I am a huge proponent of being positive and it has helped me become more successful professionally and personally. I do not think being positive by itself, will make you successful; you have to take action as well. When I say to be positive, I do not mean putting on a smile when you feel horrible inside or assuming everything will work out without any effort. I am talking about feeling happy, feeling good, and being positive about yourself while taking steps to make yourself more successful.

This chapter is about becoming successful in life by changing your attitude and actions. I am writing this chapter because an attitude change and personal coaching helped propel my life to a completely new level. It was not just one thing I did that created success, but many techniques that when used together produced amazing results. I have a real estate team of ten that helps me sell over 200 homes a year and fix-and-flip ten to fifteen homes a year. I have a wonderful family and plenty of time to spend with them. With my attitude change, I was able to start a blog, which has been an amazing experience.

WHY DOES BEING POSITIVE OR FEELING HAPPY MAKE YOU MORE SUCCESSFUL?

The idea that positive thinking can create success has been around for thousands of years. Many people might know the idea of positive thinking creating success, as the "law of attraction". The basic idea is what you think and feel will be attracted back to you. You feel happy and happy things will be come into your life, you feel negative and negative things will be attracted back to you, etc.

Many people think the law of attraction is a load of hogwash, because no one has explained the science behind the idea of positive thinking to them. Many books explain the law of attraction as a magical even. Think happy, and magic vibrations will magically come to you, bringing happy things into your life. I am not one for mysticism and magic. I am a very logical person, but I believe in positive thinking, not because of magic, but because of science.

The science of positive thinking is all about how our subconscious mind works and that our subconscious mind is much smarter than we are. Our subconscious can handle millions of tasks at once (such as keeping us alive, walking, driving, riding a bike, typing, etc.), while our conscious mind can barely handle doing a couple of things at once.

We have to teach our subconscious mind what to do and what we want. Remember how hard it was to drive a car or ride a bike when you had never done it? Once you learn how to ride a bike, you do not have to think about it, you just do it. We had to practice over and over until our subconscious learned what we were trying to do. After we complete a task enough times, it becomes ingrained into out brain and we longer have to think about it. It takes time to learn something new and teach our subconscious what we want.

The subconscious treats our thoughts the same way. If we think we are a failure or cannot do something, our subconscious will think that as well. On the other hand, if we are happy and think we are good at something, our subconscious will think we want to be happy. If our subconscious thinks we can do something, we have a better chance of doing it. If we are happy all the time, it will help us to become happy, by helping us get things or do things that made us happy in the past. That may be making more money, hanging out with friends or any number of things.

How will being positive improve your outlook and performance?

When we are happy and positive, we perform better in our lives. If you are negative and thinking about all the things that can go wrong, you will find the things that are wrong and ignore what is going right. We all know people who find the negative in everything. Even the happiest situation can turn into a horrible day, because something minor goes wrong. Likewise, we know happy people who are always enthusiastic and excited about life. Even when things seem terribly wrong, they are happy and looking forward to the future. It has been difficult for me to find contractors for my fix and flips, but I would rather have the problems of finding contractors than no properties to flip. The events that occur for people are no different in how good or bad they are, the difference comes from the person's perspective and interpretation of what is good or bad.

When you are feeling positive and happy you, are looking for positive and happy things in life. If you are looking for positive things, you will find them, and if you are looking for negative things, you will find them. When you are happy and positive, you also tend to be more alert and open to opportunity. Opportunity is all around us, we just have to have the ability to see it and go after it.

JUST BEING POSITIVE WILL NOT GET YOU WHERE YOU NEED TO BE

Being positive and happy is a great start, but it is not everything. You cannot do just one thing to be successful. You have to incorporate many habits and actions to become successful and happy. If you are happy all day long, but never set a goal, take any action, or educate yourself, you are not going to get very far. Many people do not see results when they try to be positive, because they are positive all day long sitting on their couch watching television.

BEING POSITIVE AND IGNORING WARNING SIGNS IS NOT A GOOD THING

I write about being positive a lot, and I have had some people comment that being positive about bad situations is a recipe for disaster. They are right! When I talk about being positive, I do not mean thinking every situation will work out perfectly, no matter what the facts tell you. I am talking about feeling positive about yourself, not assuming everything that happens will be positive. I like to hope for the best, but plan for the worst.

If you have a situation that is going bad or has already turned bad, you have to take action to make the situation better; it will not fix itself. While you are fixing the situation, you can still feel good about yourself. Feeling positive is not about putting a mask over your eyes to hide bad situations. It does give you the confidence to handle bad situations and find solutions.

BEING POSITIVE MAKES YOU MORE CONFIDENT AND WILLING TO TRY NEW THINGS

The biggest advantage of being positive, is it makes you feel good about yourself. When you feel good about yourself, you have confidence, and confidence allows you to try new ventures. Being successful involves risk taking, getting out of your comfort zone, and being able to act fast. Confidence makes all of those things possible, and confidence comes from being positive and feeling good about yourself.

BEING POSITIVE DOES NOT ALWAYS SHOW ON THE OUTSIDE

Many successful people show a very hard exterior. They do not smile, they do not laugh, but inside they are happy. Some people love showing a hard exterior, and that makes them happy and positive. It is not about what you show or pretend to be, it is about how you feel.

TIPS TO BE MORE POSITIVE

It is easy to be positive when things are going great; the hard part is when things are going bad. We all have things that occur in our lives that upset us or make us unhappy. The trick is to realize that we are feeling bad, then identify why we are feeling bad and do something to make us feel better. Many times just identifying why we feel bad will make us feel better. Sometimes we feel bad for the silliest or most minuscule things that do not really matter. How can you feel better about yourself?

- Make a list of all the accomplishments you are proud of in your life. Most people are surprised at how much they have done. If you want to take it a step further, record this list and listen to it when you feel down.
- Listen to motivational CDs or read a motivational book.
- Take some time off to do something fun like golf or spend time with your family. Even if you are super busy, it is important to have free time to do things you enjoy. That free time will make you feel better and might just give you the break you need to figure out how to be less busy or solve your current problems.
- Exercise or go for a walk.
- Notice how beautiful the world is around you. When I go for a drive, I try to notice the tress, the color, and the sky. We live in an amazing world.
- Listen to your favorite songs.
- Call friends or family you like to talk with.
- Remember to live in the now. You cannot change the past, you cannot predict the future. You can live for right now, and do what you can right now to fix things if they are broken. You can do the best to be as happy as you can be now, worrying won't make problems go away. Regret won't make things better. Being positive and happy right now, might help things be better in the future and give you the confidence to fix thing faster and take advantage of opportunities.

CONCLUSION

Feeling positive all the time, will not make you successful by itself. You also have to take action, set goals, get out of your comfort zone, and make things happen. At the same time, if you do all those things, but constantly tell yourself how horrible you are, and how you will never succeed, you won't succeed. You are sabotaging your hard work, by assuming things won't work out. Your subconscious thinks you don't want to succeed, because you constantly tell yourself you won't. Success takes a lot of work, you must have faith in yourself, look at the good things in your life, and attract good things back to you.

8. DO NOT LET OTHERS TELL YOU WHAT YOU WANT IN LIFE

One of the biggest mistakes I made in my life, was caring what other people thought about me. That may sound harsh, but it is true. As an introvert, I was very shy and was always worried about what others thought. I worried about how I looked, I worried about what I said, and I worried about sounding dumb. To combat these worries, I didn't talk much, especially to people I did not know. When I was younger, I was that kid hiding behind his parent's leg, anytime someone new was around. I opened up when I was around people I knew, but that was about it.

When you are constantly thinking about what others think of you, you may be scared to try new things, because you might look stupid. You may not speak up about a topic you care about, because you are worried what people will think. You may be the number one expert on a subject, but scared to teach others, because they may not believe you or think you are being smug. I think when I was growing up, I secretly wanted people to notice me. I wanted people to think highly of me, but not many did. Not because of anything I did, but because of things I did not do. If you never do anything, no one will ever commend you or notice you.

As I grew up, I became less shy and got over some of my issues. I still cared what people thought of me way too much. I think in general most people are scared to do something, until they see a lot of other people doing it. It is called the pack mentality. Once a certain number of people are doing something, it becomes a social norm and acceptable. I was very concerned with social norms, because I didn't want to look stupid or be the only one doing something. Even though I go over a lot of my shyness and I was okay talking to strangers, I still did things that I was supposed to do. I dressed very normal, I did the same things everyone else did and I tried to be "cool". After college I tried to get a normal job and go the normal route. I invested in the stock market using an IRA, because that was what everyone said to do.

When I started to invest in real estate and myself everything changed very quickly for me. I realized there were better ways to do things, than what society tells us to do. I guess when your parents say: "if everyone else jumps off a cliff, would you do it too?" has more meaning than we think. It is much easier to follow the norms, than it is to break away from them and create your own route. Standing up to people, breaking away from the pack, doing something different than all of your peers, takes courage. Most people would rather be safe, than risk doing something different. Almost everyone who is ultra-successful and who gets noticed, breaks away from the pack. You may not know what they did behind the scenes to be different, but you can bet they weren't afraid of what people thought of them.

After taking over the business, creating my own team, buying rentals and starting a blog, I thought I had graduated to the point where I was confident in myself. Then I started to seriously consider buying a Lamborghini. The point where I realized I still cared way too much about what people thought of me, was when I visited a Lamborghini dealer in Dallas. I saw Diablo, which was just a little over $100,000. I had never spent more than $40,000 on a car and that was a used Audi S4. I thought I was year's way from buying a Lamborghini, but the dealer told me they have long-term financing on exotic cars, up to 12 years. The interest rates are fairly low (under 6 percent), and the payments are relatively low as well since you are financing the car over 12 years. When I heard that, my head started spinning and I felt a little anxious. What they dealer had just told me, was I could afford this car much sooner than I ever thought. I had previously believed I would have to pay cash (whether it is smart to finance a Lamborghini we will cover later on).

The reason I was nervous and anxious, was not because I was excited, but because that was the first time I realized how close

I was to owning an exotic car. The first thought that popped into my head, was what will everyone think of me? Will they think I am giant jerk, show off, for owning such a car? I stopped myself and I knew I had a lot of work to do on myself and my attitude. If I cared so much about what other people thought, that I would let it deter me from buying a life-long dream, than I knew I needed to change my thought process.

I slowly got over caring what other people thought about me and a Lamborghini. I ended up buying one in May of 2014, which was less than a year after I visited that dealership. I will talk much more about the car later in the book, but it was an awesome decision that I have never regretted. Do some people think I am a giant jerk, show off? Probably, but many more people comment on how beautiful the car is and love seeing it. It is especially cool for people to see the car where I live in a 100,000 person town in Northern Colorado. The car was great for business, is absolutely awesome and has doubled in value! I have attended many car shows, and networked with some awesome people because of the car as well. I it is hard to believe that I thought about not buying one, because I was worried of what other people might think of me.

Before I was in a position to be able to afford the car, I had completely discounted buying one, because I never thought I could. I also listened to society which told me, regular hard working people don't every get cars like that. There is also a huge frugal movement in the United States that promotes spending as little money as possible on everything. I am not a fan of overspending, I think that saving is integral to success, but you can't deny yourself all happiness either.

The entire point of this rambling chapter, is you must figure out what you want in life, do not let others decide for you. If you want a fancy car, watch, clothes, houses, etc., find a way to get those things. Make sure you really want those things and you are not letting society or peers push you in the other direction. I see people with money smoking cigars, with massive watches and Rolls Royce's all day long. If that is

55

something that makes you truly happy, great go for it and don't let anyone stop you. If you are simply doing it to fit in with the crowd, will that make you happy? Or are you paying too much attention to what others think and possibly letting image ruin your life by overspending?

We are all different, we all have different things we love and things that make us happy. Do not let society tell you what should be cool or not cool. Figure out what you want and what makes you happy. What do you love to do? What are your favorite things, when you have free time? Do not let a lack of current resources determine what you want in life. You never know what the future has to offer, do not limit yourself to what you can afford now.

9. Why Setting Goals Will Make You More Successful in Life and Real Estate

Setting goals has helped me become more successful in life and especially in real estate. I run a real estate team of ten, I have rental properties, I fix-and-flip ten to fifteen homes a year, and I created Invest Four More. There is no way I could have accomplished all of this without setting big goals and using those goals to take action. When you figure out what you want in life, goals can help you accomplish those things. Sometimes goals will even help you figure out what you want in life. I am continuously creating goals, changing goals and tweaking what I want out of life.

I think we all want to be successful. Many of us do not know exactly what success means to us. How much money, free time, or security equals success to you? If you do not know the exact answers to these questions, it will be very hard to become successful. If you say you just want to be happy, what is happy? Is happy being able to quit your job and travel the world, or is it being able to take the occasional camping trip? You have to figure out what you want in life and you have to define it in writing. Once you know exactly what you want in life you have started to create goals.

Hopefully the chapter on being comfortable and not letting others tell you what you want in life, have helped you figure out what success means.

Why do you have to write goals for them to be effective?

Some people believe thinking about their goals is good enough, but it is not. The problem with thinking about goals, is we forget things constantly. If you have twenty different things going on in your life with work and your family, how will you remember to think about your goals? You may not even remember what your goals are!

Writing your goals helps you remember what they are, and reminds you of them. If I do not have my goals written down, I lose track of them and do not think about them. Writing your goals down also solidifies them in your mind. The actual act of writing a goal down helps you visualize it and helps imprint it in your brain. The more you think about your goals, write them down, see them, or listen to them, the better chance you have of reaching those goals.

HOW DO YOU REMEMBER TO LOOK AT YOUR GOALS?

Humans are creatures of habit and the more we do something, the better chance we have of continuing to do it. After you write your goals down, it does no good to put those goals away and never look at them again. Set aside a time to review your goals and schedule time as you would an appointment. It is best to review your most important goals daily, but you should be reviewing all of your goals on a weekly basis.

I also record my most important goals on my iPhone and listen to them every day. On my way to work, I listen to my goals and my dream story (more on that later). I like to record my goals with a long break before I hear the next goal, so that I can visualize and think about that goal before I start thinking about the next goal on the list. I also cut out a big goal and plaster it in plain sight on my fridge or garage door. I try to review all my goals as often as possible.

Any written goal is a great start, but there are ways to make your goals more effective. Goals need to tell you what you want, when you want it, and they should hold you accountable. A weak goal would be,

I want to own a Porsche.

The problem with this goal is it is excessively vague and it does not have any accountability. The goal says you want to own a Porsche, it does not say you will have one or you will buy one. There is no date when you will buy the Porsche or what kind of Porsche. If you want a 911 Turbo, but end up with a Cayenne SUV, you may not be very happy. A good goal would be, *I will own a black 1999-2001 Porsche 911 Turbo by January 2017 or sooner.*

This goal is very specific for what you want. It allows you to visualize the goal, which is very important. It also has a date for when you will buy it to hold you accountable. Notice I used the words or sooner. You do not want to limit yourself to buying that car in 2017 if you are able comfortably to do so sooner.

If you are not dead set on a Porsche 911 turbo, you could also say,

I will own a black Porsche 911 turbo or something better by January of 2016 or sooner.

WHAT SHOULD YOUR GOALS CONSIST OF?

A car may be a bad example for a great goal, because in today's society you can buy a car when you may not really be able to afford it. I happen to love cars, and many of my goals involve cars. Your goals should include anything that is important to you or that you want to do. You should not limit yourself to a few goals; you should have many goals. I took Jack Canfield coaching, which instructed me to come up with 101 goals. It was not easy to come up with that many goals. I believe the average person came up with only 56. I came up with about 80 my first try. Completing this exercise is awesome, because it forced you to think hard about what you want to do in life. It also creates big and small goals. Some goals you may be able to complete tonight, which you have been putting off for years.

59

GOALS SHOULD INCLUDE ANYTHING YOU WANT IN LIFE FROM BIG TO SMALL

- Money made in one year
- Net worth by a certain date
- Vacations: where, when?
- Special events you want to attend: Super bowl, concerts, Kentucky Derby, etc
- People you want to meet
- When you want to retire
- Where you want to live
- What your house will be like
- What cars you want
- How much you will give to charity
- What charities you will volunteer for
- What is your perfect job
- Businesses you want to start
- Relationships you want to create or make better
- Small things that you need to do but keep forgetting about

HOW REALISTIC SHOULD YOUR GOALS BE?

There are many opinions about how big and outrageous goals should be. Some feel you should not have goals that are too big, because it may not be realistic and therefore less effective. Others feel you must have big goals to challenge yourself to do better than you ever thought you could.

I have a goal to buy 100 rental houses, which is a big goal. I like big goals because I believe they make us perform better than if we had small realistic goals. The trick is you do have to believe in your goal. It will be very hard for me to buy 100 rental properties, but I also thought it would be very hard to buy a Lamborghini and I did that this summer. Buying 100 rental properties is believable for me, I know it is possible. If my goal was to buy one million rental properties by next year, that wouldn't do me much good, because I have not belief that is possible.

60

HOW CAN YOU BELIEVE IN GOALS THAT SEEM TOO BIG TO HAPPEN?

If you make big goals, you need to convince yourself they are possible. How do you make yourself believe in something that seems impossible? It is simple; you never know what the future holds for you. How  can you think something is impossible when you do not know what will happen. Now if your goal is to fly like a bird with just your arms, which may be impossible. However, if you set goals that are physically possible, such as tripling your income, that is not impossible. There is opportunity all around. You have to recognize it and go out and get it.

If you think you are not lucky enough to be rich or were not born into money, you have to change your attitude immediately. The truth is most millionaires and billionaires were not born into money; they made it themselves. If you do not believe you have the skills to make it big, think about this. The person who makes the most money usually did not invent something or create an incredible technology. The rich figure out how to do existing things better or more efficiently. You do not have to reinvent the wheel to make it big. In fact, most inventors do not make much money, because they do not know how market their product. Andrew Carnegie was a steel magnate and the richest person in the world at one time. He was a Scottish immigrant with no money to his name when he came to the US. He had no idea how to make steel, but he started working in a steel mill and learned the business. He hired great people who knew about steel and he let them grow the business for him. He was known for working few hours and taking the entire summer off to visit Scotland. You do not have to be a genius or sacrifice your life to make it big.

If you do not want to start with huge goals, at least make sure your goals challenge you and will make you work hard to reach them.

WHAT IF YOU DO NOT REACH YOUR GOALS? ARE YOU A FAILURE?

People like to claim they cannot make big goals, because they might fail and then feel bad. I do not believe in failure. You only fail if you give up and stop trying.

Goals also change. There is no rule that says you cannot change a goal after you write it down. You may find a new goal much more fulfilling and exciting than your current goals. However, That does not give you an excuse to change a goal every time you are frustrated or run into a roadblock.

I had a goal to build a loft in my old house. I worked for months to figure out a way to build that loft and nothing would work, because the house had engineered trusses and it did not make sense to rebuild the entire roof. Then my wife happened to find a better house with a bigger garage and a loft! The solution was not building a loft, but buying a new house. I found a better goal to replace the old goal.

If you have a big goal that you do not reach, you did not fail. The goal is to help you succeed and do better in life. Even if you set a big goal and do not reach it, you more than likely got much farther in your pursuit of that goal than if you had set a smaller more manageable goal. The problem with small goals is that you can accomplish them too easily. If you have a yearly income goal that is well within what you know you can make, when that goal is accomplished you will relax and stop working hard. A big goal will keep you working hard throughout the year and push you to make even more money. If you don't end up reaching that high income goal, who cares, you still made more money than you would have with a small goal. Goals are not meant to be milestones that you either accomplish or fail to reach. Goals are a tool to help you do more, and be happier.

ONCE YOU HAVE WRITTEN YOUR GOALS AND STARTED TO REVIEW THEM, WHAT IS THE NEXT STEP?

Writing your goals is the first step to making your goals become a reality. Once you write them, you have to start taking action. If you have 100 Goals, you cannot write a detailed plan for each goal. However, you can take your top three or top five goals and make a detailed plan for them. A detailed plan involves writing down what you have to do to accomplish the goal, including:

- Who you need help from
- How you will get their help
- What education you need
- What resources will you need
- How will you get those resources
- What tasks will you do every month, every week, and every day to accomplish your goal

Once you have a plan for your goal and actions you can take to reach your goal, those big goals will not seem so big anymore. You may find yourself revising your big goals, because you are accomplishing them faster than you ever imagined. I have achieved over 30 of the 101 goals I wrote down about a year and a half ago. Some of those are small goals and some are very big goals. Some of the goals I accomplished ahead of schedule and some took me a little more time than I hoped. I know one thing for sure; I would not have accomplished half of what I did, without written goals and a plan to accomplish them.

10. MY PLAN TO PURCHASE 100 RENTAL PROPERTIES

I made this goal and plan based on everything I learned from my coaching. To hold myself accountable and remind myself of my goal, I wrote it down in detail on my blog Invest Four More. Not only did I write down my goal, but it was out there for everyone to sell. This chapter is that article to show you how detailed I made my plan and what caused me to make such an aggressive goal. Some of these concepts will be talked about in more detail in this book, but I still think it is cool to read through this and see what I was thinking about at the time. I wrote this plan out in 2013 and slowly added more notes and updates on how the plan was going.

I am a big believer in making big goals and one of those goals is to purchase 100 rental properties by 2023. I have been a real estate agent and investor for more than ten years and I love the income my rental properties provide. Buying 100 rental properties will allow me to retire with more than enough money to reach my current dreams and goals.

This article is not about how to buy 100 properties quickly with no money down; it takes a lot of money, time, and effort to buy 100 properties. I only buy houses that are well below market value and have great cash flow. That is why I make so much money on my rental properties.

TO CHALLENGE MYSELF, MY GOAL HAS CHANGED FROM PURCHASING 30 RENTAL PROPERTIES TO PURCHASING 100 RENTAL PROPERTIES

In 2010, my original goal was to buy 30 rental properties in ten years. I based that goal on what I thought I could realistically achieve when I started buying rentals. A couple of years ago, I realized my goal was too easy because I knew I could buy 30 houses in ten years. I had given myself no room for improvement in my investing strategies or real estate business! At the start of 2013, I reworked all my goals including my rental property purchase schedule. My new goal is to buy 100 rental properties by January 2023, because it challenges me and will make me work hard. I had no idea when I first made this goal how I could buy 100 rental properties, but that is why we make big goals; to challenge us to do more and to change the way we do things.

WHY DO I WANT TO BUY 100 RENTAL PROPERTIES IN TEN YEARS?

I want to buy 100 rental properties because of the income and freedom that 100 houses will give me. I make over 15 percent cash on cash returns on my rentals, because I purchase them below market value. If I can buy 100 rental properties with the current cash flow requirements I have, I will make a lot of money. According to my calculations, I will be making over $900,000 a year in cash flow, have at least 60 houses paid off, and have over 11 million in equity in my rental properties. Those figures are not adjusted for inflation and assume no appreciation or rent increases. That kind of income should allow me to afford whatever my family and I want and allow us to do whatever we like. We only live once and I want to get everything that I can out of life.

The first part of this article discusses the philosophy behind buying 100 rental properties, why it is important to have big goals, and why it is important to think big. The second half of the article discusses the numbers and a detailed purchase schedule.

IS IT POSSIBLE TO BUY 100 PROPERTIES IN TEN YEARS OR LESS?

To be completely honest, I do not know how I am going to buy 100 rental properties by January 2023. I do not make nearly enough money to buy 9 or 10 houses a year. I have barely been able to buy three houses a year. I bought my first rental property in December of 2010 and I started my rental property purchase goal on that day. I should have had three by December 2011, six by December 2012, and nine by December 2013. I started out very slow buying only one rental in my first year. I have picked up speed and as of March 2016, I own 16 rentals, still behind where I had hoped to be. That does not mean I will not reach my goal. The reason I have not purchased as many rentals lately is I that have been buying many more fix and flips that have eaten up my capital. Once I get those flips sold, I will have a lot more money to invest in rentals.

Why do I think I can purchase 100 rental properties by January 2023 if I am so far away? Earlier this year, after reading and listening to books on how to become wealthy I started reworking my life goals. A couple of ideas are repeated in books and audio tapes beginning with Think and Grow Rich by Napoleon Hill. Think and Grow Rich was published in the early 20th century after Napoleon Hill followed Andrew Carnegie for decades. Carnegie was one of the richest men in the history of the world and wanted someone to study rich people in the world and write a book about how and why they became rich. Because Carnegie was one of the richest people in the world, he was able to grant Hill access to most of the world's wealthiest people. Think and Grow Rich is now known as one of the first self-help books and many of its basic ideas are still taught today by the world's most famous life coaches and teachers.

YOU HAVE TO BE POSITIVE ALL THE TIME IN ORDER TO CARRY OUT BIG GOALS SUCH AS BUYING 100 RENTAL PROPERTIES

Being positive is a theme that is repeated in every self-help book and audio recording I have ever listened too. I am a strong believer that our attitude has a huge influence on our success in life. The books range from slightly crazy to extremely scientific reasons for how being positive can greatly affect the success we have in our lives. You may have heard of the law of attraction, which states that the universe will return to us whatever we put out. If we are positive and happy, we will get positive and happy things back. If we are negative and sad, negative and sad things will come our way. I am a very logical and scientific person and was not sold on this idea right away. I had to know why this would happen. How could being positive magically bring positive things into our lives?

I started doing research on the brain and on how the law of attraction theory worked. I found out that it is not all magic; there are scientific reasons for why the law of attraction works. It is based on the subconscious part of our brain and on how it operates our bodies. We know that our conscious mind is only a fraction of what our brain is responsible for. Our subconscious mind is constantly working to keep us alive by telling our heart, lungs, muscles and the rest of our bodies what to do. Most of our movements and actions are performed by our subconscious not our conscious mind. We do not have to think about walking, talking, driving, writing, or even most of our daily tasks. By doing those things repeatedly, we have programmed our minds how to do them.

Tying this back into the positive thinking idea, if we are always thinking positively, our subconscious will think positively, too. If our subconscious thinks we are happy all the time, it will do what it can to make us happy. Why do we care what our subconscious thinks? It is much smarter than our conscious mind. The subconscious is responsible for handling millions of tasks at once while our conscious mind can only handle a handful of ideas at once. If we let our subconscious know what we want it will help guide our lives and help us to get what we want. Whether it is love, happiness, money, or material items our subconscious has much more power than we think. The theory also states that you must think about what you want, not what you do not want, because our subconscious cannot tell the difference. If you are constantly thinking about not having money, then your subconscious will do its best to make that come true as well. If you are constantly thinking of not getting sick, our subconscious will do its best to get you sick. Think of being healthy, think of being rich, and think of the good things, not the negatives.

WHY CHOOSE SUCH A BIG GOAL AS BUYING 100 RENTAL PROPERTIES?

Almost every self-help book will tell you goals are extremely important. Without goals, we have no direction, no path, and no idea of what we really want in life. There are varying ideas of how our goals should be constructed. Some say we just need broad wide-open goals such as being as happy as possible all the time to make whatever is best for you to come to you. Others say to be as specific and detailed as possible with your goals, break your goals into smaller goals, and then have a period for when those goals will be accomplished. Eventually you will have a detailed blueprint for how you will get to where you need to go.

Some people say you need realistic goals and others say you need outrageous goals. As you have probably guessed, I like outrageous goals! The reason I like outrageous goals is that they are challenging! If I know that I can reach a goal and if I know exactly how to reach it, where is the motivation for me to push myself? I want goals that make me think and reach for new ideas and systems. I have no idea what opportunities or challenges will face me in the future, so why should I limit my future goals to what I can do now. I may have a huge increase in income or find a new system that allows me to buy houses cheaper. I have such a lofty goal because I have no idea what could happen.

I WILL NEED HELP FROM OTHERS TO BUY 100 PROPERTIES

Many of the self-help books also talk about how we all need friends, co-workers, or acquaintances to help us reach our potential. Some use the term mastermind to describe groups of like-minded people who meet to help each other succeed by offering advice and motivation. The idea is that the more people to brainstorm ideas, questions, problems, etc. the better chance a great idea or solution to a problem will come about. I do not have a mastermind group, but I have recruited my best friend to work with me and learn the real estate business. He was a top-level manager in the corporate world and left his six-figure salary behind to learn real estate from me. I benefit by having a new mind to bounce ideas off and have more help in the office. He benefits by getting out of the corporate grind and learning how to be truly wealthy. He also has a flexible schedule and he is not stuck behind a desk all day.

FOCUS IS A KEY TO ACCOMPLISHING BIG GOALS

The self-help teachers also say how important it is to focus on one task or goal. All the greats had something in their mind that they really wanted. They did not let anything stop them until they got what they wanted or died trying. I have always thought of myself as being able to multitask, a jack-of-all-trades type of person. So far, it had worked out well, but I know I can do better. I know there are things I can improve in my business to make it run better and make more money. I have always thought that I knew everything about finding good deals in real estate. After starting this blog, I have realized that there is a whole world I have been missing in direct marketing to off-market properties. Instead of trying to manage five different sources of income myself, I need to delegate less important tasks to my staff and focus on the real moneymakers. If I can focus intently on a couple different areas of my work instead of just skimming over 50, I know I can improve my numbers significantly.

VISUALIZATION WILL HELP ME BUY 100 HOUSES

Many great athletes will tell you how important visualization is to succeeding in sports. Great golfers visualize exactly how their shot will look before they hit it. Basketball players repeatedly visualize hitting the game winning shot. The wealth teachers are all huge supporters of visualization. They say visualization will give your subconscious a clear picture of what you want and then your subconscious will do its best to make it happen. If you want to change your life, start visualizing how it should be every day. Better yet, go see, touch, and smell the things you want. Test-drive the car you always wanted, look at your dream home, or immerse yourself with the things you want and your subconscious will get to work. I wrote a ten-year dream story on exactly how I wanted my life to be. I described a beautiful house and in three months, I bought that house. I was not even planning to move and in no way thought I could afford a house like the one I have now, but it became a reality.

USING ALL I HAVE LEARNED TO REACH MY GOALS

Based off the ideas I have just discussed, I think I have a good chance of reaching 100 rental properties. I still do not know exactly how it will happen, but I know it will or I will find a better and more challenging goal. I have to train my subconscious to help me reach the goal. I have to be positive all the time. I have to think about my goal constantly and break it down into manageable pieces. I must have help and I have to focus more intently on my important goals. I also have to visualize myself already achieving my goals and having everything I want. Even if not all of this makes me rich, worst-case scenario, I am a positive, determined, focused person who knows exactly what he wants. *I recently bought a Lamborghini Diablo thanks to goals and visualization.*

BREAKING DOWN BIG GOALS MAKES THEM MORE REALISTIC

I have broken down other goals in my life, but I have yet to break down a goal this big! I am going to work through the goal while writing the blog and see where I end up in 9.5 years.

I wanted to write this article to help convince myself that it is possible to buy 100 properties. The first part of this article was all about my mindset. Now, let us get down to the numbers. Here is a year-by-year breakdown of how I plan to purchase 100 rental properties.

YEAR ONE OF MY PLAN TO PURCHASE 100 PROPERTIES; 2014

With my current income, I can purchase three rental properties a year and I have purchased that many in the last three years. I should be able to do a cash out refinance on at least one rental property in 2014 and get enough money to buy another property. I am also counting on my new attitude and work ideas to create enough extra income to purchase one more rental property. I also just acquired a HELOC on my personal residence for $60,000. I think that will allow me to purchase one more rental. New goal for 2014 is to purchase six long-term rentals. *Update: I bought out my parents business in September 2013, which will account for a big income jump in 2014. I sold my house and bought a new one, which eliminated the HELOC, but I gained more cash in the buyout.*

I will have 15 houses with about $9,400 in monthly cash flow. That is $112,800 a year all going toward paying off mortgages on my properties. I will have paid off one house at the beginning of 2014 and will pay off one and a half more in 2014. *Update; I paid off my first rental property in February of 2014. As of October 2014, I have 11 rental properties. I am behind, but my fix and flip business has taken off. I should have much more available capital at the end of the year to buy more rentals.*

YEAR TWO OF MY PLAN TO PURCHASE 100 PROPERTIES; 2015

In 2015, with income and savings, I should be able to purchase four properties. I should be able to do another cash out refinance and buy another rental property as well. I also believe my continuous improvements will allow more increases in income, through either listing or flipping houses. The increased income will allow me to add another rental and HELOC another as well. I am hoping the addition of my friend beginning to work with me will bring in more income from his real estate activities, which will allow another purchase. My goal for 2015 is to purchase nine rentals. *Update: In 2015 I bought five more rentals to get to 16 total*

I will have 24 houses with about $15,200 in monthly cash flow. That is $182,400 a year all going toward paying off mortgages. I will pay off the other half of one property and two more rentals in year two and will have four properties paid off.

YEAR THREE OF MY PLAN TO PURCHASE 100 PROPERTIES; 2016

I believe I will increase my income and savings enough to be able to buy five rentals. I will have 24 rentals and I should be able to refinance at least two of those properties. That will allow two more purchases and the HELOC should add the flexibly to add another rental. I am still planning to add to my income every year with increased business. This year I see a big jump in income with my friend being around for his third year and our new marketing and listing techniques taking off. I see three more rental properties being purchased from new income. My goal for 2016 is to purchase 11 rentals. *Update: Not only has my friend been selling houses but our team has also added another agent and we plan to add more.*

I will have 35 houses with about with about $22,200 in monthly cash flow. That is $266,400 a year all going to pay off mortgages. I will pay off four and a half more properties for a total of eight and half properties paid off.

YEAR FOUR OF MY PLAN TO PURCHASE 100 PROPERTIES; 2017

From my current income, I will be able to buy eight rental properties. I will continue to refinance two properties a year, which will allow at least two more purchases. I am also going to use the HELOC to buy another and I am still planning to increase my income. I am going to stay conservative and assume enough income to buy one more property this year. My goal for 2017 is to purchase 12 rental properties. *The only change I see happening is that with the increased income I may not have to refinance quite as many properties.*

I will have 47 rental properties at this point with about $31,400 in monthly cash flow. That makes $376,800 a year all going to mortgage payoff! I will pay off the half of a mortgage left over from 2016 and five more properties in 2017, making 14 properties paid off.

YEAR FIVE OF MY PLAN TO PURCHASE 100 PROPERTIES; 2018

From my current income, I will be able to purchase nine rental properties. I will refinance two more properties and use the proceeds to buy two more rentals. I may not have enough money in the HELOC this year so I will not count on that, but I will count on my income increasing enough to purchase one more rental. My goal for 2018 is to purchase 12 rental properties. *Note: to buy this many properties I will need about $300,000 in cash for repairs and down payments.*

I will have 59 rental properties with a monthly cash flow of $41,000. That makes $492,000 a year all going to mortgage payoff. I will pay off seven and half more properties in 2018 making 21.5 properties paid off.

YEAR SIX OF MY PLAN TO PURCHASE 100 PROPERTIES; 2019

From my current income, I will be able to purchase ten rental properties. I will refinance two more properties and use those proceeds to buy three more rentals. With inflation and appreciation, I should be able to refinance the properties for more money than in previous years. I will not use increased income to buy another property. If my income increases, I will use it for fun stuff such as vacations or cars! My goal for 2019 is to buy 13 rental properties. *Right on target!*

I will have 72 rental properties with a monthly cash flow of $51,600. That is $619,200 going toward mortgage payoff. I will pay off the half mortgage from 2018 and nine more properties in 2019 making 31 properties paid off.

YEAR SEVEN OF MY PLAN TO PURCHASE 100 PROPERTIES; 2020

From my current income, I will be able to buy ten rental properties. I will refinance two more properties and use that money to buy three more rentals. I will not count on any more raises in income since I do not need it at this point. My goal for 2020 is to purchase 13 rental properties. *Once again, I am counting on having enough income to reduce the amount of refinanced properties I need. I have big goals!*

I will have 85 rental properties with a monthly cash flow of $63,400. That is $760,800 a year going towards mortgage payoff. I will pay off 11 more properties in 2020 making 42 properties paid off.

YEAR EIGHT OF MY PLAN TO PURCHASE 100 PROPERTIES; 2021

From my current income, I will be able to buy ten rental properties. I will refinance two more properties again and purchase three more rentals with that money. My goal for 2021 is to purchase 13 rental properties.

I will have 98 rental properties with a monthly cash flow of 75,600. I will have $907,200 a year going towards mortgage payoff. I will pay off 14 more properties in 2021 making 56 houses paid off. *Note - I am doing all of this without using any cash flow from my rentals to buy more properties. If something changed such as finance rules, I could use cash flow to buy more proprieties.*

YEAR NINE OF MY PLAN TO PURCHASE 100 PROPERTIES; 2022

I only need to buy two more properties to reach my goal! I made it ahead of schedule and when I started writing this article, I was not sure how I would be able to reach 100 properties by 2023. I do not need to refinance any properties at this point and I can start using my income any way I want or I could retire!

I will have 100 rental properties with a monthly income of $82,400. I will have $988,800 a year going to whatever I want it to go to at this point. I can stop paying down mortgages if I want to or I could keep buying properties if I get bored. I came really close to the figures I estimated before writing this article. Falling just short of one million in income from my rental properties (which was more than I thought) and just shy of 60 properties paid off.

ASSUMPTIONS IN MY PLAN TO PURCHASE 100 RENTAL PROPERTIES

You may be wondering how I came up with my figures. To be honest I used very basic figures to make things easy on myself.

I assumed $600 in monthly cash flow per property. I am making between $500 and $700 per property now.

I assumed each mortgage that I paid off would increase monthly cash flow by $400.

I do not assume any inflation because that would cause the numbers to be much more difficult to figure!

I assume my portfolio lender will continue to lend on as many properties as I want. I will have 43 houses financed at one time and then those will start to decrease as I pay them off.

75

I assume I can continue to do cash out refinances with my portfolio lenders.

I assume interest rates will not increase significantly.

I assume rental rates will not go up.

MORE BENEFITS OF RENTAL PROPERTIES THAT MY INCOME PROJECTIONS DID NOT ACCOUNT FOR

Rental properties have great tax advantages, which I discuss here. Every rental property can be depreciated, which will save me thousands in taxes each year. I assume my rental properties will not appreciate, but they have already seen huge appreciation in the last two years, increasing my net worth by $600,000. I assume rents will not increase, but my rents have increased as well over the last couple of years. I rented my first rental property for $1,050 a month in 2011 and it now rents for $1,300 a month. I will most likely be better off than my projections indicate if I can buy 100 rental properties.

POTENTIAL ROADBLOCKS TO BUYING 100 PROPERTIES

These are many assumptions and one or more of them may not work out as I plan. However, other factors may help me do even better than I planned or balance out any roadblocks I run into.

- New ways to find properties: I am going to start direct marketing to off-market owners. This should allow me to buy properties even further below market and I may even find a few owners who will finance down payments. I recently realized I could use my IRA to buy proprieties!
- Private money: One of my goals is to find new sources of private money that will allow me to finance more

repairs and down payments. This would allow me to put less money into properties and buy them faster.

- New income sources: I have no idea what the future holds as far as opportunities and money. I may find a gold mine that will allow me to buy properties for cash and not have to worry about financing at all!
- I assume I will not do anything with the houses I pay off free and clear, but if needed to I could easily get a line of credit or refinance one of these houses to bring in enough money to buy a few new properties.

Update: One thing I did not expect happening so fast was the buy-out of the real estate business. This will drastically increase my income and buying potential. I have already begun to set up my job so I do not spend a lot of time on day-to-day tasks. My team handles most of the work for me including management of my properties.

WHAT WILL I DO IN 2023 WHEN I HAVE 100 RENTAL PROPERTIES?

I have many things I would love to do if I did not have to work. Here is a list of a few of the things I would love to do with one million dollars a year coming in and no job!

- Start a pizza restaurant
- Start a car dealership
- Travel the world with my family
- Donate time and money to those less fortunate
- Play in the World Series of Poker
- Attend a Super Bowl
- Play golf all over the world
- *Buy a Lamborghini Diablo (done!)*
- *Buy a beach house*
- *Help teach others about real estate (doing my best now)*

I have a much longer goal list than what is above and I hope to do many of these things before 2023. I know I will have time, money, and the freedom to do these things at that time.

CONCLUSION

I plan to purchase 100 rental properties by January 2023, but I realize that may not happen. If something better comes along to change my plan, I am ready to embrace fully any new opportunities. I have already changed focus slightly in 2014 to fix and flipping over buying long-term rentals. I have done this for two reasons:

1. There have been more fix and flip opportunities than rental opportunities in my market.

2. The money from flipping will help me buy more rentals; rentals take a great deal of cash.

It seemed crazy to think I could increase my income enough to buy this many properties when I first made this goal in 2013. However now that it is late 2014, I can easily see myself making more than enough money to buy 100 rental properties and have plenty of money left over to do other fun activities. At some point, I may decide it is better to buy larger multifamily buildings than single-family homes, but for now, I see more opportunity in the single-family market in my area than multifamily.

I wrote this goal out in 2013 and updated it in 2014, it is now 2016. I think goals are vitally important to achieve what you want in life. Will I reach this goal? I do not know. If I don't reach it, will I be a failure? No! I am already way ahead of where I would have been without this goal. That is the point of goals, to motivate you to go farther than you think you can.

If you are interested in rental properties I have a full length book on the subject: Build a Rental Property Empire: The no-nonsense book on finding deals, financing the right way, and managing wisely. The best Selling book is available on Amazon in Paperback or as an ebook.

http://www.amazon.com/Build-Rental-Property-Empire-no-nonsense/dp/1530663946

11.   HOW ONE THOUGHT CAN HELP YOU FOCUS AND BE SUCCESSFUL

For some reason everyone has problems finishing an important task or a big project. We lose our focus, we get distracted, we find something else to do, or we run into a roadblock that we cannot get around. Why does this seem to happen with every task that is important to us? Most likely, we have a mental block that is keeping us from finishing that super important task. How can we get around that mental block and be more successful at everything we do?

I know changing my attitude has helped me be much more successful than I ever thought possible.

ONE BOOK THAT HELPED ME BECOME MORE SUCCESSFUL WITH FOCUS

The War of Art, by Steven Pressfield, is an awesome book. My Jack Canfield coaching program recommended this book to me and it was fantastic. Steven Pressfield also wrote *The Legend of Bagger Vance* and many other successful books and screenplays. The author discusses his techniques and attitude that helped him break through his own writing blocks and succeed. The biggest thing I got out of this book was my personal slogan, "conquer the resistance".

WHY MOST PEOPLE LOSE FOCUS AND DO NOT FINISH WHAT THEY START

One of the great lessons in *The War of Art,* is to finish what we start. That sounds like a simple thing, but it is not easy to do. Think about when you have a big project for work or are close to finishing something you have worked on for a long time. When we are really close to finishing our task, we suddenly lose momentum and get distracted. A task that we should have completed long ago is still lingering around not finished.

Steven Pressfield calls this feeling resistance. He explains that when we are close to completing something great, resistance will always pop up. Resistance distracts us, makes us think the job is harder than it is, and makes the last part of any task the hardest. If I think back to the things I really am proud of, it took a lot of work at the end to get those things done. The hardest part was always crossing the finish line. The reason the last part of something is the hardest part is mostly mental. For whatever reason, when we are almost finished we relax, we stop working as hard, we assume the last part will be easy, and we get ourselves into trouble.

ONE GREAT IDEA THAT WILL HELP YOU FOCUS AND MAKE YOU MORE SUCCESSFUL

The author suggests that simply acknowledging that we are running into resistance will greatly improve our lives. If we realize that resistance will come to us in almost everything we do, we will realize resistance is something to push through and defeat. Instead of lagging, finding other things to do, and putting off finishing our tasks, we will push harder at the end to conquer the resistance and finish that task.

HOW CAN YOU USE THE IDEA OF RESISTANCE TO BE MORE SUCCESSFUL?

I loved this book because it helped me do so many things better. Whenever I become frustrated, feel like I hit a wall, or am stuck in a rut, I think about resistance. I ask myself if I am really stuck or if resistance is causing me imaginary problems? I love using resistance to give me more motivation with almost everything in my life. Besides real estate related problems, I use resistance when I work out, with my personal life, and even with toys that I want. I like to lift weights, and when I think about conquering the resistance, I always lift more. So much of what we do is mental and you really see it when doing something physical like lifting. The idea of resistance has helped with many other tasks.

- **Blogging**: When I get frustrated with the growth of my blog or bugs, I think about resistance and pushing through the down times.
- **Dealing with ten fix and flips at one time**: contractors have caused me plenty of headaches and pushing through to hire more has been something that will help my business going forward.
- **Dealing with twins**: I do not have to explain that one.
- **Taking over a business**: There have been many hurdles I have had to overcome taking over the business from my father
- **Running a team of ten**: They do not run themselves, and no matter how much help I hire, I still have to make sure they are doing the right things

WHY I CREATED MY OWN PERSONAL SLOGAN

After reading *The War of Art*, I kept thinking to myself, "Conquer the resistance"! I said it enough that I decided it should be my own personal slogan. I actually wanted it plastered on my home office wall, which my wife did as a present! Now when I work on things in my office I see the slogan and it reminds me that I can get through anything.

CONCLUSION

Once I started pushing harder at the end of a project or task, things have become much easier in life. Those tasks that were hanging over my head, were now completed and I did not have to think about them anymore. Instead of having ten different things half done, I had a couple of things I was working on, and I made sure I completed the tasks that should have been done.

12. THE MOST SUCCESSFUL PEOPLE NEVER STOP LEARNING AND EDUCATING THEMSELVES

The most educated and successful people in the world never stop learning. They may have graduated from school a long time ago, but the learning continues forever. The most educated people are not always successful, but if you couple education with hard work and goal setting, it can create awesome results.

Being successful does not mean you stop learning and educating yourself. Some people become successful, and they may start to think they know it all and do not need any more classes or seminars. Some people feel it is a sign of weakness to seek help. I never read self-help books or listened to educational CDs until a couple of years ago. I was guilty of thinking I was too good to learn anything from those books or CDs. The most successful people in the world realize there will always be people they can learn from, they never know everything and they can always get more education.

WHY IS EDUCATION IMPORTANT TO HELP PEOPLE SUCCEED?

It is imperative we let others help us and educate us about anything in life. It may be possible to learn something ourselves, but why not use thousands of years of human experiments to see what is the best way to do something? For almost every task imaginable, there is a book or article about the best way to do something. The guidance we can get from other's experience is priceless. Even if you want to add your unique style or create a better way to do something, you can build on what others have done. You do not have to start from scratch when there is so much information available.

HOW CAN PEOPLE CONTINUE TO EDUCATE THEMSELVES?

When we first think of education and learning, we think of school: high school, college, trade school. However, there are many ways to learn besides going to school. I attend a couple of real estate conferences a year and I always learn so much. I do not just learn from the classes or speakers, but from agents I talk to and companies that attend the conferences. We can learn just as much from people in our business as we can from school. We have to have an open mind when talking to others. We have to listen and be aware that we may not know everything, and other people may have a better way to do things. Books, websites, and seminars are a great way to learn new information as well. You do have to remember that not everything you read or see online will be correct.

WHY DO PEOPLE HESITATE TO EDUCATE THEMSELVES?

I used to think there was something special about doing things myself without help or guidance. I thought being self-taught somehow made what I was doing better than if I had help.

When looking back at why I thought being self-taught was better, I was building in excuses in case I did not succeed. If someone was better than I was at something I could say, "I was self-taught and that person had lessons". Our egos stop us from seeking help because it might show weakness, or we are not as good or special as we thought. When we are talking about life, the best of the best always have coaches and they educate themselves constantly.

Is it better to have help and be the best you can be at something, or to be self-taught and be pretty good? When it comes to business, life, and being happy, I want to be the best I can be. If it takes help to get there, I am just fine with that.

THE BEST OF THE BEST NEVER STOP LEARNING

The best professional athletes are not always the most talented. They are the athletes who are the most coachable and work the hardest. The richest people in the world are not necessarily the smartest people with brilliant ideas. They have learned from others and have hired the best people to work for them. The richest people may not always have a great formal education, but they have mentors and people who have taught them how to succeed. The most successful people are constantly learning and adapting. They never stop learning or listening to people, even when they reach the top of their profession or business.

HOW CAN YOU CONTINUE TO LEARN YOUR ENTIRE LIFE?

When you first hear that you need to continue to learn your entire life, it may seem overwhelming. When do I get to relax and take a break? Remember the chapter on being comfortable? Challenges and learning should be fun. When you are excited about learning, you are learning about something that you love or that is at least interesting and fun to learn. When you learn how to motivate yourself and look at life as a challenge and not a bunch of problems, you will look at learning the same way.

HOW HAS EDUCATION HELPED MY REAL ESTATE BUSINESS?

I started a blog, *Invest Four More*, in March of 2013. At the time, I thought I knew pretty much everything about real estate investing. I had been very successful and learned a lot from my dad about selling real estate and fix and flips. My plan with the blog was to help others learn about investing, not to learn myself.

I did help educate people about real estate investing, but I also learned more about real estate and my business than I thought possible. I learned about direct marketing, better ways to rent houses, better ways to flip houses and much more. I learned how to write better, how to market better, and how to create a successful blog. Luckily, I was open to learning and became more successful by writing the blog.

YOU HAVE TO KEEP LEARNING TO BECOME THE BEST YOU CAN BE

Our school system is set up for students to go K-12 and then college. We then have a choice to continue our education with more college. Once we are done with college, we start working. Many people stop learning when they start working, but you must continue to learn, maybe even more so than when in school. When you start working, you have a job and know exactly what your responsibilities are. You should be researching the best way to complete your work, going to seminars to learn from the best in the business, and learning from people you work with. The more you learn, the farther you will get in your job. You may see more opportunities in other jobs or you may see the value in working for yourself.

It is important to remember that we never know everything. When you stop learning, you stop advancing and most likely, others who are not afraid to learn will pass you up. I constantly read and listen to audio tapes as well as attend conferences and seminars. I know I do not know everything and I never will. I think rental properties are a great investment and selling real estate is an awesome way to make a living. However, I am not going to limit myself to real estate if I see greater opportunities in something else.

LEARNING AND EDUCATING YOURSELF IS NOT LIMITED TO WORK

Jim Rohn said we must work harder on ourselves than on our work. When you learn to work harder on yourself than you do your job, money will take care of itself. I believe this as well: if you are a successful person, what you do is not that important. You can make money and be successful doing anything. Being open-minded to self-help books, audio CDs, and personal coaching has helped me improve my personal life more than my business. I took personal coaching to make more money and it ended up changing my entire life. It gave me more free time, more confidence, more control, and more money. The money seems to come once you are in the right mindset and have the right attitude. Do not forget to educate yourself about how to make yourself better, not just your work.

HOW MUCH MONEY SHOULD YOU SPEND ON EDUCATION?

There is a tricky balance between spending money on education that is worthwhile, and spending all your money on education without ever taking action. The most educated people in the world, may not ever be successful if they never take action. The truth is, if you are serious about education and learning you will spend a lot of money on education, but the actions you take based on that education should more than make up for the money you spend. The trick to spending your money wisely, is making sure you spend your money on things that will help you.

When deciding where to spend your money, watch out for bait and switch techniques. There are many people looking to take advantage of motivated individuals by making big promises with big price tags. If someone lures you in with a free seminar that turns into a $20,000 course to get the real information, it is probably a scam. If you do not learn anything in the first seminar except you need to buy more classes to learn more information, be cautious!

Some courses and education, especially personal coaching can be expensive. However, real programs will not try to trick you into buying them; they will tell you the costs and benefits upfront. There is no bait and switch and you do not have to keep buying more classes to get the real secrets.

I buy books and audio CDs all the time. I see no problem spending money on books, because one piece of information could be well worth the price of the book and most likely much more. Self-help teachers suggest people spend as much as ten percent of their income on personal improvement. I do not spend this much, but I do spend thousands a year on educating myself about personal and business improvements.

CONCLUSION

Once you get into the mindset of constantly learning and improving any way you can, life becomes a lot of fun. When life becomes a challenge and not problem after problem, success will come. Do not be afraid to learn from those who have had success. Be the best you can be and get as much from life as possible!

13. THERE IS NO SUBSTITUTE FOR HARD WORK AND DEEP WORK

Up to this point the book has been about strategies and attitudes to help you succeed. No matter what you do, you will have to work hard. There is no substitute for hard work. Sitting on the couch all day, practicing these techniques will not make you successful. If you implement the techniques in this book, I think it would be almost impossible to sit on the couch all, day because the techniques should force you to take action. There are arguments about life-balance and if it is possible to have a balanced life and be ultra-successful. It think you can have life balance, but the life balance may not be working 9-5 every weekday and never working the evenings or weekends. I believe life balance means working hard, but also making sure you have time for the things you love and for your family. You may have to work non-stop for a week, but then take the next week off. When you do work, you have to be extremely focused and very efficient. Too many people in today's world, show up for work, but don't actually work. They check email, they browse the internet, and they talk to co-workers. If you want to be successful and have a life, you cannot screw around when you are working. You have to be working hard, not just show up. Deep work is a concept I read about in a book called, you guessed it, Deep Work. It is the concept of working without distraction for long periods of time. The author suggests those who can master deep work in a society with so many distractions will have a huge advantage and be very successful.

THERE IS NO SUBSTITUTE FOR HARD WORK

When I was struggling early in my career, I was not working crazy hours. I was actually trying to figure out ways to work less, by utilizing technology and other people. The problem with this strategy, is I had not found much success yet. In the beginning, you have to work hard and you may have to work long hours. When I started to get a lot of REO work in the real estate business, I had to work 12 hour days, weekends and it was stressful, but it was also awesome. I knew I was accomplishing things and going to make some money. Working that much, actually felt great. I knew I was doing what most people are not willing to do and I was building something. I also knew I could not work that much forever and be happy. But it was fun building something and putting everything I had into it. If you want to be successful, and not just above average successful, but really successful you have to work hard and put everything you have into it. When I worked that many hours, I had to focus because I had so much to do. I had to be very careful with my time, because it was so valuable. It was a blessing, because it taught me how much time I was wasting personally and professionally.

The Four Hour Work Week is an awesome book, which taught me a lot about delegating and hiring people. The book is about delegating tasks and freeing up your time. I that all the time now and get a lot done because I delegate. We can't always start out working few hours, delegating everything and make a fortune. In the beginning you may have to work long hours, sacrifice time with friends and hobbies to get to where you want to be. You may not have any money to hire people in the beginning either. Starting a successful business or career, does not come easily. Some of the most successful entrepreneurs I know, have crazy work ethics that they acquired through athletics or the military. They do not quit or give up, until they have accomplished what they set out to accomplish.

SUCCESS MAY NOT COME QUICKLY

Many people are able to work hard for a short period of time. A few days, maybe a few weeks or even a few months. Success usually does not happen quickly. It takes time to lay the groundwork, perfect the processes and see the results of your hard work. I talk to people all the time who are incredibly motivated for a day or two. They quickly realize that real estate or whatever they want to do, will not produce quick results, so they jump to something else. The new venture does not produce quick results, so they jump to something else. They keep jumping to new opportunities until years have passed and they have nothing to show for it.

Working a few 12 hour days, may not be enough to get to where you want to be. It takes a lot of hard work and it takes time. If you do not have the stamina to stick out a plan, a business idea, a new venture, you are probably wasting your time trying it. Before you start something, give yourself a realistic time frame for how long you will work it, and work it hard.

WHAT DOES DEEP WORK MEAN?

Deep Work is a book that I recently read, and it was awesome. The idea is that when you work, you must be fully immersed in that work with no distractions if you want to do the best job possible. It is argued that many of the worlds "geniuses", were not born that way, but became that way by the way they worked. If you want to figure out complicated math problems, understand a novel written in another time, or write an amazing business plan, you cannot complete those tasks while talking to other people, checking email or browsing the internet.

The author goes to explain that deep work is not simply working 30 minutes at a time without looking at email. It is working for hours at a time, without thinking about or working on anything else except the task at hand. In order to produce extraordinary work, one must focus intently on the task at hand without any distraction. That means no phone, no email, no computer, no television and no visitors. By completing tasks in this way it trains your brain to focus more intently, do better work and figure out things that would be impossible the way most people work. This is something that is extremely tough for me. I have people in my office all the time. I have a home office, but it is tough to find time away from the family to complete work without distraction. I am really bad about checking email and my phone. However, I completely agree with the idea that deep work can be life changing and most people cannot or will not do what it takes to make deep work happen.

I will go into focus more in the book, but I wanted to mention this concept because it shows you what your ultimate goal should be when you work. Many people work very early in the morning or late at night to avoid distraction. When you are short on time, have too much work for the hours in the day, you have to be focused to make every minute count. When you are forced to compete a task in a certain amount of time, we can usually do that, but it takes focus and we have to say no to people and other less important tasks. If you can get to a point where you treat all of your work this way. Focus on one thing at a time until it is done. Eliminate all non-essential conversations and distractions. Give all of your brain power to one thing at a time, you will get so much more done in the time you have. That is why sometimes it is good to work 12 hour days or 80 hour weeks, because it forces you to make changes that will improve the way you work. More focus, less distractions, better work.

Not only might it take more hours than a normal job to get started, it will take more focus as well. If you can someone manage to eliminate distraction and work long hours, you may get more accomplished in one year, than most people could accomplish in three or more.

14. HOW TO MANAGE YOUR TIME BETTER

In the last chapter I talked about deep work and working hard to get what you want in life. I also mentioned you have to work smart and not just a lot of hours. How can you use your time better?

We concentrate on doing our jobs and running our business, but many times ignore the best way to make more money. If you had more time in your life, you could easily make more money. We all have a finite amount of time given to us, we can't add hours to the day no matter how much money we have. We have projects in the back of our minds, better techniques to implement at work, or research we would love to do, if we had more time. If you can figure out how to manage your time better, you can make more money and enjoy life more!

There are multiple ways to manage your time better and make more money. Make sure you use that extra time wisely. If you blow all your extra time watching television, it is not going to do you much good. There are some simple ways you can increase the amount of time you have.

THE MORE FREE TIME YOU HAVE, THE MORE MONEY YOU CAN MAKE

The more time you have, the more money you can make and the more money you make, the more free time you should have. In my opinion it is much easier to take steps to increase your available time, than to increase the money you make. Many people make the mistake of mismanaging their time, even after they have made enough money to last the rest of their lives. All the money in the world does you no good, if you have no time to enjoy it. Manage your time better now and you will be able to live life to its fullest.

HOW DOES FREE TIME ALLOW YOU TO MAKE MORE MONEY?

You may be asking how in the world free time can equal more money. There are a lot of unemployed people with tons of free time not making any money. If you have too much time and not enough to do, you need to look at your life and make some big changes. The world is full of opportunity and ways to educate yourself or make more money. If you find yourself bored, with nothing to do, and wanting more money, do something. Get off your butt and do something. Research ways to make money, exciting things to do or a business to start. Think about what you really love to do and find a way to do it more. If you own a business, have a full-time job, or even a home maker, most of us are short on time. If we had more time we could pursue a new career, a new source of income or pursue a hobby.

All of these pursuits can lead to more money and more happiness. Pursuing a hobby means you are doing something you love. If you love doing something, there is a great chance you will be successful at it and be happier! I have a huge list of business ideas and ways to add sources of income to my current business. My biggest problem is finding time for everything. Between my job, my blog and my family it does not leave a lot of extra time. Thanks to my coaching I have been able to decrease the amount of time I spend on my job and increase the time I spend on new pursuits and my family. Every time I gain free time, I am able to fill it up with a new opportunity or venture and almost immediately make more money. How have I been able to increase my free time and make more money?

1. INCREASE YOUR TIME BY IMPROVING CONCENTRATION
I enrolled in Jack Canfield life coaching at the start of 2013. One of the principles of the coaching program, was learning how to focus on one task at a time. Our society promotes multi-tasking and doing eight things at once. I know I was

guilty of multi-tasking all the time. I would check my email every five seconds, answer my phone every five minutes and constantly switch between tasks. The fact is when you are switching between tasks constantly it takes longer to compete those tasks. Every time you switch tasks, it takes time to figure out where you left off on a task, where to find information or paperwork on another task and to remember all the tasks you are trying to complete. Multi-tasking is not a good thing.

I have learned to concentrate on one task at a time, until that task is completed or a set amount of time has passed. I don't check email, I don't answer my phone, and I concentrate on that one task. I will be the first to admit it is hard to do. I constantly want to check email or switch between tasks, but I make myself concentrate on one task. This saves me a lot of time over the week and I complete my tasks at a higher level of quality. Focus, has allowed me to manage my time better.

2. SCHEDULE EVERYTHING TO INCREASE FREE TIME
Another technique I have learned from coaching was to schedule everything, even though scheduling is very hard for me. I took the Myers Briggs personality test and it said I like things to change constantly. I don't like the same routine over and over, I guess that is why I love real estate. That personality trait makes it very hard for me to schedule my day, let alone my week.

I have been scheduling more and more and I am able to manage my time better through scheduling. The reason scheduling saves time, is you have a plan for the day or week. You don't waste time thinking about what needs done or if you will have enough time for everything. One great technique is planning the next day, the evening before you go to work. If you know exactly what to start working on, you won't waste half an hour getting settled in and deciding what needs done first. If you have your day planned out, you are able to manage your time better and make more money.

3. NEVER WORK BELOW YOUR INCOME LEVEL-DELEGATE

The most important thing I learned in coaching, was to never work below my income level. This is an extremely difficult thing for many people to do. The idea is to hire out any work that can be done for less than what your time is worth. Calculate what your time is worth per hour based on your income level. If you are worth $100 an hour, don't mow your lawn when you can hire someone to do it for $40 an hour. Use that extra time on money-making activities that earn $100 an hour or spend it with your family. If you run a business, don't bog yourself down with busy work that someone can do for $15 an hour.

Being busy does not equal being successful. Hire someone to help with the busy work and tasks you don't like. It will make you happier and allow you to make more money, because you are focusing on the money-making activities.

4. MANAGE YOUR EMAIL AND PHONE

Another great tip I received through coaching, was how to handle email and phone calls. I am a REO broker and I do most of my work through email. I have to check my email frequently because my clients require it, but I don't have to check it constantly. If possible set out chunks of your day for checking email. Email can eat up huge chunks of time if you check it every five minutes. Always take care of the most important emails first. Then work your way down to the least important and try to save personal emails for after work.

My phone rings all the time during working hours and many times during non-working hours as well. If I were to answer every call, I would spend half of my day on the phone. My coach suggested I change my voicemail to let people know when I will return calls. On my voicemail message I tell people to text or email me for the fastest response. If they leave a voicemail I will return it between 10 and 11 or 3 and 4. Most people know to email or text me and it saves a ton of time! If I call someone on the phone, it takes at least three minutes and could take much longer. An email or text response takes me about 15 seconds.

One exception to this rule is I have the most important numbers for asset managers saved in my phone. I answer those calls or return their messages ASAP because they make me more money!

5. EAT THAT FROG IS A GREAT BOOK AND IDEA
Eat That Frog, is a book on how to save time in your day and stop procrastinating. The basic premise is to eat that frog first, which means to do the most difficult and dreadful task first. By doing the most difficult task first, it eases your mind and makes the rest of the day much easier. Manage your time better by not procrastinating!

Another great book that helps with procrastination is the War of Art. It talks a lot about distractions in our society and how to avoid them and get work done. The book talks about resistance and this term has helped me tremendously. Resistance, is that thing that keeps us from competing a task, finishing that paper, or pushing through to finish something really important in our life. Do you ever notice how a really big task is always hardest at the very end when you think you are almost done? It is hard to finish with the same enthusiasm you started with and the same quality. The War of Art calls this resistance and if you can recognize it, it can change your life. "Conquering the resistance" has helped me break through those difficult tasks and even work out harder and more often.

6. TIME BUDGET IS A GREAT WAY TO SAVE TIME
With a time budget, list all your activities during the week and how much time you spend on them. List out the most important activities and the least important. Take a good look at what you are spending time on and if the majority of your time is spent on the most important things. For work, don't block out 8 hours a day and forget about it. Break down those

8 hours into exactly what you are doing and what are the most important tasks. Then try to plan your next day or week using that time budget. Allocate a certain amount of time for family, job, hobbies, sleep, eating etc.

7. WHAT IF YOU HAVE A CORPORATE JOB?

Many of these techniques work best if you own your own business. If you work for someone else or are in the corporate world, they can still be utilized. The Four Hour Work Week, is a great book on learning how to delegate and use your time better. The author had a regular job and ended up outsourcing almost all of his work for much less money than he made. This allowed him to pursue other interests and start his own company with his free time. I would advise anyone who tries this to consult with their boss before outsourcing their work. I don't want you to get fired. The author Timothy Farris, ended up with a business that earned him $80,000 a month. In his business he does basically nothing, it runs better without him being involved.

Even if you aren't able to outsource your job, you can use these techniques to improve productivity and that will get you noticed. Getting noticed usually leads to promotions and more money. The worst case scenario, is you manage your time better and have more free time to pursue other money-making activities.

8. TOO PERFECT IS ANOTHER GREAT BOOK AND INFLUENCE

Too Perfect, is another book that changed my life. It is about obsessive compulsive traits in people and how it affects our lives. When my coach first had me read it, I thought I am not obsessive compulsive, this is a waste of time. Then I read the first chapter and realized there is a lot more to being obsessive compulsive than being a clean freak or a complete over the top compulsive. I realized I have a lot of obsessive compulsive personally traits.

- I always think about work

- I have a hard time relaxing completely
- I want tasks at work done perfect, not matter how important they are
- I always want to get the best deal and I worry about the quality of completed work.

I realized these are traits are found in most good businessman. I also realized many good businessman focus on work and seriously lack quality family time or me time.

The second part of the book talks about how to be less compulsive and relax. I realized not every task has to be perfect. I can concentrate on the most important tasks, not spend too much time on the less important tasks and not worry about the past (completed tasks). Not only have these changes reduced stress and anxiety, they have increased my time. The better I manage my time, the more money I make!

9. MAKE A LIST OF EVERYTHING YOU HAVE TO DO
It is so simple, yet many people don't write down what they need to do for the day. The less time you think you have, the more important it is to make a list of everything you need to do. If you have it all written down, it is much harder to forget a task. When you get super busy, it is also easy to get anxious and overwhelmed. When I get anxious and overwhelmed, the quality of my work suffers and I make more mistakes. I always make sure I have a list of tasks and once I look at that list I realize "I can do this" and get to work. I take a deep breath, focus on one task at a time and very rarely do I not get everything done. I manage my time better by writing everything down and making as many lists as I can.

CONCLUSION
You should have noticed some common themes in this article. The more relaxed you are, the better you work and more you get done. The more organized you are, the more work you get done. The more you schedule and the more you concentrate on

one task, the more work you get done. The more you delegate the more work you will get done. If you get more work done, you have more free time. Manage your time better. The more time you have to focus on money-making activities and you will make more money!

15.   WHY TAKING TIME OFF FROM YOUR BUSINESS OR WORK WILL MAKE YOU MORE SUCCESSFUL

It takes a lot of hard work to be successful, but being successful is not all about hard work. Being successful involves planning, goal setting, getting out of your comfort zone and in some cases taking time off. To get ahead in life you may have to work more than 40 hours a week. However, you cannot spend all your time working, because you will burn out and miss out on life. You may even be missing inspiration that could make you even more successful.

WHAT IS THE MOST IMPORTANT REASON TO TAKE MORE TIME OFF?

This chapter is not for people who have no problem taking time off. Success usually comes with hard work and if you are not willing to work hard to achieve your goals, you will never reach them. This chapter is for those that have learned that success comes from hard work, but have a hard time getting away from work. They are either constantly working or thinking about work to the point where work runs their lives.

The most obvious reason to take time off is to spend time with people you love. How many times have people lost the respect of those around them because they spent all their time working? It is easy to convince yourself that you are doing what is best for everyone by working and providing for your family. I am not saying you should not work hard or work long hours, but you cannot work all the time. Your family may say it is okay and they understand the work, but are they telling you how they really feel? Some of the most important time we can spend with our children is when they are young; you do not want to miss that because you were gone constantly.

Being successful is very important to many people, but is it more important than your family? To some people it may be, but to me it is not. I have set up my business so that I work about 40 hours a week, sometimes less, sometimes a little more. When I first became very successful in real estate, I was working much longer hours. My wife understood I was going through a transaction and had to work those long hours, but I made changes so that I could work less and see my family more often.

When I had to work long hours, I still tried to be home for dinner so that I could spend time with my wife and kids. I would go home at five or six, spend a few hours at home and then go back to the office when my kids went to sleep. This was not the most efficient way to work, because I spent time driving back and forth and it takes time to transition back into work mode. However, I thought it was much more important to spend time at home than to work nonstop.

WHEN YOU STOP WORKING, STOP THINKING ABOUT WORK AS WELL

When you finish working for the day, do not continue to think about work all evening and into the night. I know there are things that come up that you will have to do, but you cannot always be in work mode. If you are still thinking about work, you are not paying attention to your family and that may frustrate them more than if you were not home and still at the office. I know it is hard in today's society to stop thinking about work when you are excited and motivated. We have smart phones, tablets, laptops, and even televisions that keep us connected at all hours of the day. It is hard for me to put my phone down and not check my email constantly, but I make myself do it. If I check my email for a minute, I may end up responding to emails for thirty minutes while I am supposed to be playing with my kids. My children are only four, but they still know when I am paying attention to them.

When I do pay full attention to my family, they are happier. My wife is happier and my kids are happier which makes me happier. Being happy is great, but I also think it makes us more successful to be positive. When we are happy it is much easier to be positive. Being happier is not the only way taking time off from work will make you more successful.

HOW WILL TAKING TIME OFF FROM WORK MAKE YOU MORE SUCCESSFUL?

I wrote earlier about the subconscious mind and using our subconscious to help us be more successful. In order for our subconscious to help us achieve more, we have to listen to it. If we are constantly working and thinking about work, we never have time to think about the big picture and get big ideas.

Our subconscious can process much more information than our conscious mind. Our subconscious runs our vital organs and remembers statistics and motor skills, while our conscious mind has a hard time rubbing our belly and patting our head at the same time. Our subconscious also stores all the information we see, hear, touch, and think about. Our subconscious is smarter than we are and we must let it help us succeed. If we are constantly working and thinking, we never give our subconscious time to help us. When we quiet our mind, stop thinking about work, and relax, our subconscious has a chance to tell us what to do.

I always seem to get my best ideas for my business on the weekends or when I am on vacation. I mentioned not looking at my phone when I am in non-work mode, but I do keep it handy if I get a great idea. I take many notes on my phone and when I thing about a way to improve my business I make a note in my phone. Our brain can forget a new idea in 37 seconds and that idea may never come to us again, so I make sure I record my ideas.

My best ideas come when I am not thinking about work. I will be playing with my kids, camping with the family, or on a beach somewhere and will get an idea that I know will make me more successful. The ideas are not brilliant observations, but usually simple things that I had not thought of before. I usually am not thinking about work when I get these ideas. It has to be my subconscious telling me what to do after finally getting a chance to speak its mind.

HOW CAN MEDITATION HELP YOU BECOME MORE SUCCESSFUL?

When I go on vacation I get really good ideas; the less I think about work, the better ideas I get. I think this is why mediation produces great results for some people and can provide huge breakthroughs. The basic idea of mediation is to clear all thoughts from your head and think of nothing. It is hard to think of nothing. Our mind constantly wants to fill our head with thoughts. If you can quiet your thoughts and think of nothing, you give your subconscious a chance to speak up. After I am able to think of nothing for a long enough time, more random, deeper thoughts come to me, which on occasion are business related and help me become more successful. Other times they make no sense, but it is very interesting to see where the mind goes.

HIRING A TEAM HAS MADE ME MUCH MORE SUCCESSFUL BECAUSE I HAVE MORE FREE TIME AND MORE TIME TO THINK

When I started listing REO and HUD homes, I became very busy. I had no time for fix and flips, rentals, or even my family. I had to make changes and those changes involved hiring more people to help me. I hired an assistant who started as part-time and then became full-time. Then another agent joined our team and we kept growing. Having a team allowed me to stop doing busy work and concentrate on the business. I started to fix and flip more houses, buy rentals, and start *InvestFourMore.com*. I had more free time with my family and I no longer had to work while on vacation! The more free time I have, the more great ideas I get and the more successful I become.

105

CONCLUSION

It takes hard work and long hours to become successful. However, you do not have to work long hours for the rest of your life and you do not have to work all the time. If you work all the time, that leaves no time for your family and no time to think about the big picture and what is important. It is okay to take time off and not think about work; in fact, it will help you become more successful.

If you can complete deep work you will be ahead in life and do great work. When you are not working concentrate on being present. When you are not working, use the same techniques you did with work. Eliminate the distractions, concentrate on the now and being with your loved ones.

16. DON'T STRESS OUT IF YOU CAN'T DO EVERYTHING

I cover a lot of ground in this book. As you can see it is not a bunch of fluff about feelings and anecdotal stories. These are real life scenarios that I have been through and techniques that the most successful people in the world use. I have a feeling many of you are thinking: how can I ever do all of this? Don't worry you do not have to get everything right away and change your life in one week. It takes time to implement these changes and time to build habits. I do not do all of this, because there is a lot to do! I like to think that as long as I am making progress every day, I am on the right track.

When I took my coaching or I read a great book, I do not implement every strategy right away. It takes me time to think about what I learned, make some changes and form habits. I find when I try to change too many things at once, I get frustrated and may not implement anything. But if I focus on one or two changes at time, I have a much better chance of those changes sticking and lasting. It is the same concept I talk about with business. Many people see me with four or five major sources of income and thing they should try to create four sources of income all at once. I did not create my business in one day and I focused on one business at a time, until I mastered it. Maybe master is the wrong word, because I am always learning new things and implementing new strategies. I stabilized one business before I started a new one.

I feel it is much better to be a master of one technique than have a little knowledge about 20 techniques. No one wants to work with someone who is okay at doing 20 different things, but not great at anything. The usually don't care about the 20 other things you can do, they want someone who is great at the one thing they need help with. Use that same strategy with yourself and improving your attitude or routines. Do not try to change everything at once and do a few different techniques once in a while. Master one technique, build it into your routines and once that is done, move on to new techniques.

If you are frustrated, anxious and feel there is too much to do. Take a step back. Concentrate on one or two things you want to improve on and work on those. If it helps, put this book a way from a while so you don't get overwhelmed. You can always read it again late. Or read the entire book to get an overview, then go back and focus on a chapter or two to implement.

17. HOW A DAILY ROUTINE WILL MAKE YOU MORE SUCCESSFUL

I covered many techniques and thrown out many things someone can do to be more successful. Keeping track of all these things can be tough. As I just mentioned, you do not have to do everything at once. But even when you master some habits, and start making progress, you may forget things or start to lose some of the habits that make you successful. A daily routine is one way to keep track of your habits and keep the momentum of what works. I have used techniques that were a huge help to me personally or professionally that I slowly stopped using, because it was easier to drift back to the old way of doing things. It takes effort to keep doing things the right way, especially when you make big changes. A daily routine will help you keep focus and remember to take of yourself before anything else.

WHAT IS A DAILY ROUTINE?

I learned how to create and perform a daily routine after taking Jack Canfields personal coaching program. A daily routine is time you set aside to review goals, review your day, plan your next day, meditate, relax, or do whatever you feel helps your life the most. A daily routine should happen every day at a similar time without distractions. A daily routine can take fifteen minutes or an hour or more, but is time for you and only you.

Many people make goals and plans and have great expectations for their business and their lives. The problem is they get distracted and stop thinking about those goals, plans, and expectations. One reason people forget about these things is they work so hard on their business, they forget to work on themselves and look at the big picture.

A daily routine helps you take a step back, stop working, and review where you are, what is working and what is not, where you are now and where you want to be. Most importantly, it helps you focus and stay on track with what is most important in your life.

How do you complete a daily routine?

There is no set way to perform a daily routine, but here are some basic guidelines to help you create one.

- Set a time that you will complete your daily routine. I do mine at 10:30 at night or close to it. It can be in the morning or at night, but it works best at the beginning or end of the day. Some people will even have routines in the morning and at night.
- Do it every day. If you start to miss a day here or there, that turns into two days, and that turns into a week. Soon you are not doing your daily routine at all. I have an alert on my phone to remind me to do my routine every night.
- Write down what you will do during your routine. I have a list that I review every routine so I do not miss anything.
- Tell your spouse and family you will be unavailable during this time. Explain why you will be unavailable and how this will help you and ultimately them.
- Create or dedicate a space for your routine. It can be a home office or any quiet space without distractions.
- Do not use the television or your laptop unless it is part of your routine. This is your time without distraction.
- Do not use your phone, do not check email, do not work, this is time for yourself.

What do I do in my daily routine?

I have the same basic task I do every night in my routine, but some nights I add a few more tasks. My basic tasks are the following:

- **Write in my thankful journal**. I have a journal where I record what I am thankful for every day.
- **Listen to my phone recordings**. I record many

things to help me remember my goals and what is important.

- **Review my big goals**. I have five to ten big goals written that I focus on.
- **Mediation**. I mediate for five to fifteen minutes to clear my mind, learn to focus, and relax.
- **Additional tasks**. I also record messages on my phone, work on specific goals, or read a small portion of a book. I do not do these every night.

WHY IS IT IMPORTANT TO WRITE DOWN WHAT I AM THANKFUL FOR?

I have a lot to be thankful for and the more I remind myself of the things I am thankful for, the happier I am. I am a strong believer that the happier I am the more successful I will be. Every night I write in my journal what I am thankful for that day, or what happened that day that made me thankful. This not only reminds me to be happy for everything I have and the people in my life, but it helps me review my day.

WHY IS IT IMPORTANT TO LISTEN TO RECORDINGS ON MY PHONE?

I have written many dream stories about how I want my life to be in the future. I became hooked on dream stories when I bought almost the exact same house from the first dream story I wrote. I was planning to buy my dream house in ten years and it took about six months. I write these dream stories down and I record them on my phone so I can constantly remind myself how I want my life to be and what is important to me. The Lamborghini was also in one of my dream stories and came much quicker than I ever imagined.

I also record my most important goals that I want to achieve or any important reminders to myself. It is easier for me to listen to these recordings while I am driving than to review them on paper all the time.

WHY IS IT IMPORTANT TO REVIEW GOALS?

Many people set goals, but most people do not achieve their goals. The reason we do not achieve our goals is we forget about them almost as soon as we set them. If you set a goal to make $100,000 in 2017, but never review that goal or take any action to achieve that goal, you will not reach it. The more you see or think about your goals, the more action you will take towards reaching them. A daily routine helps me review my goals constantly and keep them fresh in my mind.

WHY IS MEDITATION IMPORTANT?

Meditation is not for everyone, but I highly suggest you try it. I mediate for about fifteen minutes every day. All I do is close my eyes, relax, and try to think of nothing. It is not easy to do if you have never tried it. Our minds are constantly thinking random thoughts; quieting your mind is not easy. Once you learn to quiet your thoughts, it is extremely relaxing. Many times when I stop thinking about everything going on in my life I come up with my best ideas and most insightful thoughts. It also calms me down if I had a bad day or something is bothering me.

CONCLUSION

A daily routine is hard to do and hard to do every day. It is very easy to let a couple of nights slip by and then stop completing your routine at all. I had this happen to me recently. I lost a lot of focus and I forgot many of my big goals. I also had some rough times business wise during this time. Maybe it was a coincidence, but I feel that keeping with my daily routine helps me be much more successful and stay on track. It also reminds me of the big picture and what is most important in my life. Creating and completing a daily routine has been one of the best things I have done in the last two years to help me become more successful.

18.   Networking and Positive Influences

You may have heard the saying you are who you hang out with. What this means, is you will be as successful as your closest friends or the people you hang out with the most often. Some even go as far as to say that your income will be the average of the five people you spend the most time with (outside of your family). I have not found this to be true for me, but I definitely see the value in networking and spending time with the most successful people you can. One of the biggest perks of buying a Lamborghini was the connections it allowed me to make online and in my area. The car attracts people who have similar cars, it lets people know I have reached a certain amount of success and it is a rare car. The Diablo is not the common choice for people who simply want a Lamborghini. The Diablo is a V-12, manual transmission car that is intimidating to drive, hard to find and not easy to maintain. If you only want a Lamborghini to say you have a Lamborghini, most people will buy a Gallardo. They are easier to drive, less expensive, more common, and easier to work on. When people see I have a Diablo they know I am a car guy and I didn't get a Lamborghini just to show off. Having that car has allowed me to network with many high level people in my area.

ARE RICH PEOPLE EVIL?

Most people I know who are successful are very positive. They have a positive outlook on life and they have a lot of self-confidence. For the most part, they are fun to be around and they are interesting. There are exceptions to every rule, but in general the rich are happier. There have been multiple studies done in the last five years, which confirm the more money you have, the happier you are likely to be. That makes sense to me, but some still argue that being rich jades people and the rich are selfish evil people. This may sound harsh. But I feel most people who promote these ideas are scared to try to be rich themselves or feel they will never be rich, so they make themselves feel better by convincing themselves they don't want to be rich.

If you are someone who feels the rich are evil, you are reading the wrong book! I want you to think about why you think they are bad people. Is it because you were taught that growing up, because you convinced yourself of that, or is it because of personal experience? Most people who feel money does evil things to people do not get that way from personal experience. It is from hearsay or things they were taught by people who were not rich. Look back and try to figure out why you have a negative feeling towards people with money. Sometimes it is plain jealousy. I used to feel that way as well. I would see someone with a nice car or house and think that must be nice. I wonder how they lucked into that money. The truth is most people with money made it themselves, they did not inherit it or luck into it. Instead feeling jealous or envious of people with money, I now look to them as motivators. I try to figure out what they did to make their money and see if there is anything I can learn from them. I talk to them, I try to make friends with them and soak up as much information as I can.

Another thing to consider when looking at your view of money and the rich, is how it affects your own success. If you constantly bad mouth people with money or are jealous of those with more, you are telling your own subconscious that you don't want money. If you think the rich are evil, you are flat out telling yourself you don't ever want to be rich. If you think the only way the rich get their money was to luck into it, you are telling yourself you can't be rich, unless you luck into it as well. These are very negative and damaging thoughts to be putting into your head.

Do not think badly of money or the wealthy, or it will be very tough to ever be wealthy yourself.

WHY DO YOU WANT TO NETWORK WITH THE WEALTHY?

There are many reasons to network. It builds relationships, give you information and can advance your business or career. There are certain people who can help you or hurt you when you network with them. Usually, the more successful someone is, the better contact they will be and the more they will help you. The wealthy may be able to invest with you, conduct business with your business or introduce you to other wealthy people. One of the most important things a wealthy or successful person can do, is teach you how to be wealthy or successful.

Whether we like it or not, when we hang around people enough we tend to start acting like them. Sometimes if I am interacting with someone from another country with an accent, I may even find myself starting to subconsciously talk like them a little! I feel pretty stupid when I find myself doing that, because I don't want the other person to think I am making fun of them, but it has happened. When our friends are negative, we tend to be more negative ourselves. As parents we are very concerned about who our children hang out with, because we know how a bad influencer can affect our children's choices and behaviors. The same thing happens with adults. If we have a bad influence in our life, we cannot expect our own choices not to be affected by that bad influence.

You can learn a lot about success from hanging out with successful people.

- How to conduct yourself: Some successful people wear fancy clothes and others wear shorts and flip flops. But, most successful people conduct themselves a certain way, by respecting people and being pleasant.
- How to manage your time: Successful people rarely waste time. One of my friends will spend a good amount of time with people, but when he has something to do or is out of time he is very clear about. He usually says: well good seeing you, I'll be in touch in at such and such time, bye. He is polite, but very clear that he is out of time and done talking for now. There

115

are people who will suck your time if you let them. You need to be in control of your time and not let others take it.

- Work ethic: Most successful people have a strong work ethic, and they do what they say they are going to do. If they say they will be there to meet you, they won't forget and waste your time. If they need to get a job done, they will do it.
- They don't have much fear: You don't see many successful people afraid to talk to others or put themselves out there. Actually, they may be afraid, but they do not let that fear stop them, they push through it.

HOW DO YOU MEET AND HANG OUT WITH THE RIGHT PEOPLE?

If you want your life to be a certain way, hang with people who have the life you want, or are at least the closest to the life you want. If you want to be a billionaire, it may not be easy to hang out with Bill Gates. You still have a choice in who you hang out with.

- You can choose to hang out with the co-worker who is always going above and beyond, instead of the co-worker who always complains about that other co-worker being a suck up and sell out.
- You can choose to hang out with the guys partying every night and working for the weekend or the people who are going to business school at night.
- You can choose to hang with the people who constantly complain about politics, the government and everything they possibly can, or the people who are thankful for what they have and constantly looking to improve.

The choice of who you hang out with, is not all about how much money they have. It is about how they see themselves, how they see the world, what their attitude is like, and if they

116

are helping you succeed with their demeanor or hurting it. While you may not be able to hang out with Bill Gates, you can choose to hang out with the positive hard-worker or Debbie Downer who blames everyone else for her problems.

Eventually you will meet wealthy people. The better you do finically, the better attitude you have, the more successful people you will meet. You cannot be afraid of them, or afraid to ask them questions. They are people just like you and the chances are good that at some point in their life, they did not have a lot of money.

19.   HOW CAN YOU SAVE MONEY?

One of the hardest parts of getting ahead in life is saving enough money. I like to invest my money in rental properties and they are expensive. There are ways to buy rental properties with little money down, but these techniques usually make it harder to cash flow than putting twenty percent down. Putting little money down also involves buying as an owner occupant in many cases, which is not easy to do for those with families. The most profitable way to buy rental properties is to put twenty percent down, make repairs, and have money in a reserve for maintenance and vacancies. However, it is not easy to save the money needed to pay for all the expenses that come with buying a rental property with twenty percent down.

No matter what line of work you are in, or what you want to invest in, you need to save money. Too many people are looking for the easy way to make it big. Usually making it big requires sacrifice, discipline and hard work. The more money you can save, the better off you will be no matter what you are doing.

WHAT IS THE EASIEST WAY TO SAVE MORE MONEY?

I can say this from personal experience; the easiest way to save more money is to make more money. Many personal finance experts suggest saving as much as fifty percent of your income. That is very hard to do if you do not make much money and hard to do even when you do make a lot of money. Our society and economy is based on consumer's spending money and it is tough to save. Making more money makes it easier to save if you do not raise your spending habits with your additional income. So many people automatically start spending money when they get a raise or a bonus.

I am not saying that you should never increase your spending habits. I am not a frugal person. I think it is good to spend money on things that make us happy. Before you start increasing your spending habits, save money and save a lot of it. The more money you save, the better off you will be financially, whether you invest in real estate or something else. If you have investments and money saved, you will feel better about spending money on things that really make you happy.

HOW CAN YOU MAKE MORE MONEY?

- **Start a business**. When you own your own business, you have control and a lot more opportunity to make more money. I am a real estate agent. I run my own real estate team, fix-and-flip houses, run a blog, and have rental properties, which are also a business. Make sure, when you start a business that you run the business and do not let it run you. The point is for the business to make money without you, not for you to work 80 hours a week doing everything yourself.
- **Ask for it**. The easiest way to make more money is ask for it. Ask for a raise if you are in a position where you work for someone else. You had better be able to justify your raise from work performance. If you have no basis to ask for a raise, start working harder and smarter and show your value.
- **Change careers**. Have you reached a ceiling in your current field of employment? Do you hate your current field of employment? Are you burned out and not doing as good a job as you should? Think about changing career paths to something you may actually enjoy.
- **Educate yourself**. The most successful people never stop learning. They take classes, seminars, read, and listen to audio books. Do not be afraid to go back to school if that will give your career a boost.
- **Do something you love**. There are varying opinions on doing something you love versus being paid. Some say it is impossible to do what you love and make money in some fields. I think anyone can make money in any field doing what they love. If you had wanted to be a professional baseball player, it may not be the exact job you had envisioned. However, that does not

mean you cannot make money in that field. You could work as a trainer, coach, manager, or product designer. When you love what you do, you have more passion and work harder at what you do. You are not watching the clock for quitting time every day because you cannot wait to leave. You are excited to go to work every day and are disappointed when you run out of time to work because you are having so much fun.

Whatever you do to start making money, make sure you set goals. Set goals and plan how you will make more money, because it will not happen without hard work and change. Go out and make things happen, do not wait for success to come to you.

THE FIRST STEP TO SAVING MONEY IS TO USE A BUDGET

I hope that you find a way to make more money, but you also need to spend less. The first way to spend less money is to realize how you are spending your money. A budget starts by tracking everything you spend money on; food, clothes, gas, housing, cars, entertainment, travel, etc. Most people never track their expenses, because they are afraid to see what they spend their money on or they are worried they will have to spend less money on things they love.

By tracking your spending, you will see a few things right away that you can save money on. You may be spending too much money on housing, food, clothing, or entertainment. Once you see what you spend, use a budget to limit your spending each month. Cutting back just a little on some expenses will go a long way toward helping you save the money you need. A great tool for tracking the money you spend and your net worth is Personal Capital. They offer a free app that links all your accounts and tells you what you are worth and what you spend.

PAY YOURSELF FIRST WHEN YOU SAVE MONEY

Unless you make a lot of money, it is very hard to get to a point where you can save fifty percent of your income. Your first goal should be to save more money than you are now. A good rule of thumb is to save at least ten percent of your income, but you should work to increase that number as much as possible.

Pay yourself first by saving ten percent or whatever percent you choose of your income before you pay any bills. As soon as you get your paycheck, put ten percent in a savings account to use only for investing. Make yourself live on what you have left after you have set aside your savings.

SAVE MONEY BY SPENDING LESS ON YOUR HOUSE

Lenders will tell you exactly how much house you can qualify for when you talk to them about getting a loan. However, qualifying for and affording a house payment are two different things. If you purchase the most expensive house you can qualify for, it will make it very tough to save any money. It will also make it very difficult to buy a rental property because you have maxed out how much you can qualify for. I like spend about ten percent of my income on my house payment, which leaves me plenty of money to save. That is not easy to do if you do not make a lot of money. Spend more on your house if you have to, but try not to buy the most expensive house you can afford.

QUICK TIPS TO SAVE MONEY

There are many books out there on saving money; I highly suggest you read them. I do not know every technique and I cannot go over everything in one chapter, but hopefully this helps you start saving more than you are now, which is the only way to start.

- Pay off credit card debt by paying of the lowest balances first.
- Compare rates on insurance. Check different companies for rates and move all policies to one

company to get a multi-policy discount.

- Eliminate or shop around for cable and cell phone services. Many times simply calling the company you currently use will lower your bill. Threaten to leave and they may give you a better price. Another option is to eliminate cable all together.
- Turn the temperature in your house down a couple of degrees in the winter and up a couple of degrees in the summer to save on heating and cooling.
- Carpool to work, walk, or ride a bike on short trips that do not require a car.
- Stop drinking or smoking and do not go out to eat every night.
- Use credit cards to pay for everything. Yes, I said use credit cards for everything, but you must be extremely disciplined. I have a credit card that pays me two percent cash back on every purchase. If I pay my balance off every month, I am charged no interest. It is like getting two percent off everything I buy and it adds up.

CONCLUSION

There are many ways to save money that I have not listed, but the important thing is to start saving now. If you can combine spending less money with making more money, you will be surprised how fast things can change. I am not a fan of being overly frugal and never spending money on anything, but you cannot spend all your money either. You need to find a happy medium that works for you where you are saving money, spending money on things that are important to you, and building a future.

20.   CAN BEING TOO FRUGAL MAKE IT HARDER TO BE SUCCESSFUL?

Saving money is great, but some have the opposite problem than could actually hurt them. There has been a huge push to live frugally in the last few years. I believe the idea to save money and invest it, is a great way for people to get ahead in life. Many people have goals to retire early, and saving a lot of money at an early age is the best way to retire early. Living frugal is one way to save money, but is living too frugally actually hurting you just as much as it is helping you? I have been frugal most of my life in many ways, but in some areas of my life I am the complete opposite of frugal. I bought a Lamborghini in 2014 and most people would think that was a giant waste of money on the surface and the opposite of frugal. In retrospect it has been an awesome investment for my business and the car has been an awesome investment itself.

While living frugally will save you money, I think living too frugal can hurt how much money you actually make. It can also damage your mental attitude towards your own self-worth and deny you happiness.

- I spend money on the things that save me time, because time is my most valuable asset.
- I spend money on things that make me truly happy or my family happy, because we only live one life and I want to take full advantage of it.
- I spend money on products, classes and education that will improve myself or my business.
- I don't spend money on things I don't care about just to keep up with the Jones.
- I don't spend so much money that I have nothing to save or invest.

- When I first started my businesses I spent very little money on myself so that I would have the capital available to grow quickly.

WHAT DOES IT MEAN TO LIVE FRUGAL?

Here is the definition of frugal from http://dictionary.reference.com/browse/frugal.

1. Eonomical in use or expenditure; prudently saving or sparing; not wasteful:

2. Entailing little expense; requiring few resources; meager; sc anty:

The first definition makes perfect sense to me. Being prudent in the way you spend money and not wasting money when you do not have too. The second definition is when people start going too far and harming themselves more than they help. The words meager and scanty are not good words. I don't want to live a meager life, but I think many people get so far onto the frugal train they get obsessed with saving and forget to live.

ARE THERE GOOD AND BAD WAYS TO LIVE FRUGAL?

While it is good to save and not be wasteful with your money, it is not good to spend money on nothing and live a meager life. For example: If you have one child and drive an Excursion to school and work every single day, it might make sense to look into buying a smaller more economical car. You have to look at why you bought the Excursion. Was it a status symbol? Was it what all your friends have? Was it the nicest car you could qualify for? Could you buy a cheaper car that gets better gas mileage and be just as happy? Or could you be even happier by using the money you save on gas and payments for something else? This to me is looking at things in a frugally good way.

On the other hand you might have to commute to work every day 15 miles and currently own a Prius. However, you are thinking about selling your Prius and using the train to commute or riding your bike. It will take you an hour longer to get to and from work. You may save a couple hundred dollars a month, but you also lose 40 hours a month in time! Maybe that sacrifice is worth it if you have no family and love to ride a bike. Is saving as much money as humanly possible in every aspect of your life worth it?

HOW CAN LIVING FRUGAL HELP YOU RETIRE EARLY?

To retire early you have to save a lot of money, invest it wisely and control your spending habits. Living frugal will help you retire early, but you can't rely on just living frugal to retire early. It is pretty obvious that saving money is a good thing, but there is more to retirement. Once you save that money you must invest in something that will make that money grow. I think real estate is the best way to make money grow quickly, but there are many ways to invest. The more money you can save, the more you can invest and the faster you can retire.

If you are looking for a site to help you live frugally, I am probably the wrong person to listen too. Mr Money Mustache has a great blog on living frugal, although I think he may take frugality a little too far and he thought buying a Lamborghini was about the dumbest thing anyone could do.

HOW CAN LIVING TOO FRUGAL HURT YOUR ABILITY TO SAVE MONEY AND RETIRE EARLY?

While it may seem obvious that saving more money can help you retire faster, is it possible that being too frugal will hamper your saving? Saving is a huge part of retiring, but you can't just look at how much money you save on each activity or thing you buy. You have to look at how much you save in your bank account. You may be saving $10 on groceries by going to three different stores, but how much time is that costing you?

You have to look at the opportunity cost when you are trying to save money. Many of us own a business or are self-employed. If you work for someone else you know what your hourly wage is or what your salary is. We should all have some idea of how much our time is worth. Most of us know if we work a little more we will most likely make more money. Even if you are salaried and don't get paid by the hour, the more you work the better chance you have of getting promoted.

I don't think working as much as humanly possible is a good idea, but we all need a certain amount of time off, time with our families and sleep. If you are spending hours each week to save money, that means you are taking time away from something else in your life. Either you are sacrificing time with family, yourself, work or both. While you may be saving $50 a week, what is the time it takes you to save that worth? Maybe it is worth it and maybe it is not. Too many people think just because they are saving money it is worthwhile at all costs.

While you may be saving $50 here or $100 there, the time it takes you to save may be costing you thousands of dollars. Sometimes it is worth it to spend a little more money to save a lot of time. When I used to plan a vacation I would spend hours looking for the best prices on hotels and air fare. I would scour the internet for great deals and end up picking the cheapest flight I could. Many times the flight had a connection, while a non-stop flight was only a $100 more. I would add hours and hours of flying time and headaches to save $100. I could be using that travel time to enjoy more vacation time and I would probably feel better on my vacation the less time it takes me to travel. If I was going on a business trip I could spend more time focusing on business and less traveling for a mere $100.

HOW CAN BEING TOO FRUGAL HURT YOUR ABILITY TO MAKE MORE MONEY AND RETIRE EARLY?

If you are unwilling to spend money on things that make you happy, are you sacrificing your happiness in the name of being frugal? We all have different likes, dislikes and hobbies. Some people like traveling, some outdoor activities, some like cars, some like clothes, and some like socializing. I don't judge people on what they like or dislike, but I think many people determine what they should or should not like based on what it costs. I like cars and I have liked them since I was a very young child. When I was younger I always wanted a Lamborghini, but when I got older I was convinced spending $100,000 plus on a car was a horrible idea. I also thought I would never have the money to own a Lamborghini. I justified to myself that it was okay to bury that desire, because I might not ever have the ability to own a Lamborghini and I didn't want to fail or be disappointed.

Hiding you true desires, wants and needs is not healthy and I think being frugal causes many people to hide what they really want in life. This attitude harms people in two ways.

If you hide what you really want in life, can you ever be truly happy? The happier people are the more successful they are. If you don't think you are worth it or will ever be able to afford the things you truly want, you will be less successful in life as well. Our sub conscious tries to help us get what we want. If you hide what you really want, you will never get it.

Big goals can be extremely motivating. When I finally allowed myself to want a Lamborghini again, my life changed. I realized I was hiding something huge that I had always wanted. When I made a goal to buy a Lamborghini I started making more money, I became more motivated and I felt different. I was happier and felt more myself that ever before.

If you don't think you are worthy of expensive things that make you happy, you will most likely never make a lot of money. If you don't have big goals to motivate you, you most likely will never make a lot of money. While being frugal will help you save, if you are too frugal it may hurt your ability to make more money. What we are really after is saving the most amount of money possible. Spending less money is one way to save, but making more money is another way to save. The biggest problem with being too frugal is what it does to our attitude and how we view ourselves.

HOW CAN YOU CREATE A FRUGAL SAVING STRATEGY?

So how do you know when you are being too frugal or not frugal enough? There is no right answer to this question because everyone is different. I try to spend money on things that truly make me happy. I don't buy things on a whim and I make sure I research big purchases. One thing I love to do is set goals for big purchases. When I do this, I will buy this. This way I make sure I save enough money, buy enough rentals or accomplish something else before I spend a lot of money. This also helps stop me from spending too much money until I have saved enough or made enough.

For my business I make sure I have enough cash available for operations and expansions. But I also am not afraid to spend money on things or education that will make more money. I talk to a lot of people who are worried about spending money on their own education, because they feel they can get the same results by learning things on their own. I was the same way when I was younger and you have to ask yourself if the extra time it takes and mistakes you will make on your own are worth it. Or is it better to learn from someone who has done what you want to do, has made the mistakes already and can drastically reduce the learning curve?

I have spent a lot of money on coaching and improving my business. It is scary shelling out thousands of dollars when there is no guarantee you will succeed. However when you spend money it also tends to give you more motivation, because you want to get your money's worth. Many times the success of the student does not depend on the teacher, but how hard the student is willing to work.

CONCLUSION

Too retire early you have to save money and make money. Some of the most frugal people in the world are often people who make very little money. Sure you may be able to retire early if you spend almost no money, but is that really how you want to live? Are you hiding and burying true wants and desires in order to live cheap? The interesting thing is that letting those desires come through and using them as goals may allow you to make more money, save more money and retire even earlier than being too frugal.

21. HOW DO YOU KNOW WHEN TO SPEND MONEY INSTEAD OF INVEST OR SAVE?

To get ahead in life you have to save money and invest money. However, at some point, you have to spend money on yourself. All the saving and investing does you no good if you never use the money for anything. I love to set goals for income and for investing, but I also set goals for things I want and things that will make me happy. In fact, the goals I set for things that make me happy are more effective than the goals for income and investing. While saving money is vitally important to getting ahead in life, so is spending money. The big question is when do you decide to take some savings or extra income and spend it on something that makes you happy instead of investing it?

MOST PEOPLE SPEND TOO MUCH MONEY ON THINGS THAT "MAKE THEM HAPPY"

It is difficult deciding when it is okay to spend money on you instead of investing. The fact that you are asking this question means that you are far ahead of the average person. Almost 75 percent of Americans have no savings and live paycheck to paycheck. If you are living paycheck to paycheck with no savings, you should not be worrying about spending money on extras right now. You should be worrying about building an emergency fund and saving money.

The first step to getting ahead financially is saving money and investing it. Many people look to get ahead by using creative financing to buy homes with little money down. You can start investing in real estate with little money down, but if you have no savings, it is much riskier. If you have rental properties, you need to have reserves to cover maintenance and vacancies. Investing in real estate with no savings and no money is asking for a disaster that would put you in an even worse financial position.

I think we all know people who buy brand new cars every two years, have a boat, a nice house, and no savings or investments. I am not saying it is bad to spend money on nice things, but saving and investing must come first. I am also not saying you need to be frugal your entire life; I am far from frugal! You have to make sure that the things you spend money on really make you happy and you are not just buying them to keep up with the Jones' or because you feel it is what you are "supposed to do". It takes sacrifices to get ahead and the sooner you make those sacrifices, the better off you will be. Here are a few examples of how I lived coming out of college.

- I drove a 1991 Ford Mustang Convertible for almost seven years as my daily driver. The car had no heat and I had to bundle up in the winter!
- I have never bought a new car. Yes, I have spent a lot of money on cars, but the newest car I ever bought was three years old.
- I never had a car loan until I was 29.
- I have never financed furniture, electronics, boats, etc., unless it was a special zero percent interest rate, and I could have paid cash.
- My first house payment was about 28 percent of my income and that was a huge mistake. It made it hard for me to save money and get ahead. After I sold my first house, every personal house since then has had a payment of less than 10 percent of my income.

If you do not save and invest enough now, you risk running into financial problems and never being able to afford the things you really want in life.

WHY DO YOU NEED TO SPEND MONEY ON YOURSELF?

Once you have saved money and invested money, you need to think about things that make you happy. If you save and invest too much without ever spending money on yourself, you risk losing your true self. You risk living your life to save instead of living to do what you really want. If you give yourself goals that make you happy, such as buying your dream house or dream car, you have a better chance of being successful. Giving yourself big goals that excite you and that you can visualize provide a huge amount of motivation.

I made a goal of buying a Lamborghini in 2014. Every day for most of 2014 while I drove to work, I imagined I was driving a Lamborghini and I bought one four months later! Not only did I find a great deal on a 1999 Diablo, but also the car has gone up in value since I bought it. That motivation helped me work harder and smarter. How do you decide when you are ready to start spending a little and stop saving everything? My solution is to give yourself targets or goals for when you can spend money. If you give yourself rewards for reaching certain milestones you will not feel guilty when you spend money, you will feel proud because buying something special means that you accomplished a big goal. By accomplishing a big goal, you also know you will be able to afford what you bought.

WHERE DO YOU START WHEN DECIDING HOW TO REWARD YOURSELF?

In order to figure out how and when to reward yourself, you have to know what you want in life. When I took Jack Canfield coaching, I had to make 100 goals. Making those goals or trying to come up with those goals (it is not easy to make 100 goals) taught me a lot about what I wanted in life. Too many people never take the time to figure out what they really want. When I made my goals, I was given instructions not to limit what I wanted based on what I believed I could achieve. Even with these instructions, I still held back on what I really wanted in life.

I made my first goals based on what I thought I could afford or what I thought I had time to do. When I started to run out of ideas for goals, I started to challenge myself and write some goals that were a little more unbelievable. After I made those goals, I started to achieve goals, including some of the goals that were less believable. It was the less believable goals that stuck in my head and I kept thinking about. The less believable goals were also the goals that made me the most excited like buying my dream house and a Lamborghini.

I went from thinking I could buy a Lamborghini in maybe 20 years if I was lucky to buying one in about a year. I also bought my dream house within 6 months of writing those goals. It was not magic that writing 100 goals made me successful; I had already been making goals and striving to become successful. The 100-goal task was the final straw that made everything fall into place and helped me believe that I could accomplish much more than I ever thought I could. Keep in mind, when I bought these rather expensive items, I made sure I could afford them!

HOW DO YOU KNOW WHEN YOU CAN AFFORD EXPENSIVE PURCHASES?

When I started investing in rental properties, I made a deal with myself that I would buy a new car when I bought my tenth rental property, not a new daily driver, but a special car that would stay in my collection. I have a plan to buy 100 rental properties and if I give myself little rewards for making progress on that plan, I think I have a better chance of accomplishing it. I bought my tenth rental property in early 2014 and I actually decided not to reward myself yet.

I was making $5,000 a month from my rental properties, but I still did not feel comfortable buying a $100,000 plus car. When I had first made the deal with myself to buy a car when I hit ten rentals, I was not even considering buying a Lamborghini. I was thinking I would buy something like a $30,000 Toyota Supra twin turbo or something similar. I decided to give myself another criterion for buying the

Lamborghini. When the blog produced enough income to pay for the monthly expenses (including the car payment for the Lamborghini) I would start seriously looking. I hit that in early 2014 as well and I still did not start looking, because it just seemed too crazy to buy a Lamborghini! Then I saw the perfect car come up for sale and I showed it to my wife. She actually encouraged me and reminded me that I had already met the goals I set for myself and I should look into buying it.

On a side, I financed the car, but I could have paid cash for it. I financed it to get a 12-year loan, with 15 percent down and a 5 percent interest rate. Instead of paying cash for the car, I could use the cash I saved to buy more rentals! When I bought my dream house in 2013, I had never considered buying such an expensive house. We had purchased the house we were living in at the time at a trustee sale and it was an awesome deal. We had $100,000 in equity, even after refinancing, that covered the down payment on the new house. I realized our payment would be higher, but still only 10 percent of our income, which meant we could easily save money after buying the house. I did not set goals or milestones for buying my dream house, but I made sure I could afford it and still save money.

WAS IT WORTH SPENDING MONEY ON A LAMBORGHINI AND BIG HOUSE?

For me it was well worth it to buy a Lamborghini and our dream home. For others with different goals, it may not be worth it or you may have other things that make you happy. I am a car nut; I have loved cars since I was three and I have always wanted a Lamborghini. I drive the car about three times a week if the weather is nice, and people love it! It is a great way for me to get into a conversation with people wherever I go, the gas station, car wash, etc. People ask me what I do. I mention I am a real estate agent and I hand out many business cards. The car has also attracted more visits to the blog and drawn more attention to our real estate team, which in turn has allowed us to bring on more agents.

All of this was a bonus. Just having and driving the car was well worth it to me. For my birthday this year, I took a one-day trip to the dealership in Seattle where I bought my car. They had a 1989 Lamborghini Countach. The owner was kind enough to give me a ride in the Countach during a rainstorm. The Countach is another car I would love to have, but at $369,000, it is a bit out of my budget and I would be scared to drive it. Below is a video of my trip and of my Diablo as well.

The house has been a great experience as well. We now have family dinners and birthdays at our home, more friends come over, and people stay longer! My wife is happy as well, which is really all that matters.

SPENDING MONEY ON OTHERS

Perhaps the most satisfying thing you can do is spend money on others. This last Christmas we adopted a couple families in the area and bought them all gifts that they could not afford. We took our time choosing families that we thought were deserving and it was a great experience for our family and for our children.

I became a corporate sponsor for the local food bank this year and it was amazing how happy they were. It was also amazing to see how many families they could feed with the money they receive.

I even volunteered the Lamborghini for Make-a-Wish and Wounded Warriors in case they have someone with a dream of riding in one. There have been no takers yet, but if you can use what you have to help others, it is a wonderful thing to do.

The more money you have, the more you can give to others. The more money you have, the more time you should have as well. Time is perhaps the most valuable thing you can donate.

DO I HAVE FUTURE GOALS AND ASPIRATIONS?

I really love our house and I would not be upset if we never moved again. That does not mean I do not give myself more milestones and goals to achieve. I admit it has been harder since I bought the Lamborghini to get as excited about new goals. I still do my best to push myself and create new and exciting things to shoot for. After visiting Seattle, I realized how awesome it would be to have my own exotic car dealership. I have also always wanted to fix up an old plantation house. Both of those goals would take a lot of money and I would have to step my game up to an entirely new level. Those goals may seem out of reach now, but so did the Lamborghini a couple of years ago.

CONCLUSION

Making big goals for yourself that you can visualize and that excite you are one key to being successful. Even if you just beginning you're investing career and trying to save every penny you can, it does not hurt to make big goals for the future. It also does not hurt to make smaller goals for reaching milestones, such as saving $5,000 or buying your first rental property. Just make sure the rewards do not cost more than the goals!

PART II: REAL WORLD APPLICATION OF WHAT YOU HAVE LEARNED IN THIS BOOK

So far we have talked about many strategies for becoming successful, using your time better, and being happier. I have given some examples of how these techniques have improved my life, but part II of the book will be about things I have done, mistakes I have made and how to best use these techniques

22. THE BIGGEST MISTAKES I HAVE MADE AND WHAT I LEARNED FROM THEM

In my blog I help people learn about real estate by sharing what has worked well for me. Many times you can learn more from mistakes than from success, and I have made a lot of mistakes! Those mistakes may have been more valuable than any success I have had. Mistakes are not something you should be ashamed of, but something to help you learn and do better next time. Many people are afraid to try something new, because they may be bad at it or fail. The truth is most people are bad at new things and it takes time to get good at something. The best way to become proficient at anything is to do it and learn from experience what works and what does not. You can learn a lot from my mistakes, but you are still going to have to take chances and make your own mistakes to become successful at anything.

THE BIGGEST MISTAKE I MADE IN REAL ESTATE WAS HAVING NO PLAN

When I became a Realtor I was lucky that my father was an agent and could teach me the business. I got a head start over many new agents by having a great mentor. However, I think joining my father's team also hurt me and stunted my growth. My father had a great system that he did very well with, but it wasn't for me. I tried to make that system work for years, but my heart was not in it and I never took any initiative to create a plan or system. I did not have to create a plan, because I was making a living and nothing was forcing me to take action. If I had been a brand new agent with no help; I may have taken action to create a plan and system much sooner because I had no other choice.

Once I had a plan, something to get excited about and a clear vision of what I wanted I had great success. The plan I chose was to become a REO and BPO agent. I don't know if the path of becoming a REO agent was the most important decision I made or the act of planning and vision of something was more important. I had no vision and no idea what I wanted out of real estate when I first started. Once I had a vision and plan I had great success and it has continued.

My number one mistake was waiting for something to happen to me, instead of making it happen. I thought I would automatically be successful without a definite plan or vision. Once I had a vision and plan I had more success than I dreamed of. I learned how important it is to make goals and have a vision for where you want to be in the future.

THE SECOND BIGGEST MISTAKE WAS TRYING TO COMPLETE REPAIRS ON A FIX AND FLIP MYSELF

That fix and flip cost me thousands and thousands of dollars and it was a huge mistake doing the work myself. It took me three times as long as it should have to fix the house and I didn't do as good of a job as a pro would have done. That decision cost me time, caused frustration and killed the rest of my business. From that point forward I always used a contractor to repair my rentals and fix and flips. Time is money and if you use up all of your time trying to save a few bucks, you are actually costing yourself much more money than you are trying to save.

THE THIRD BIGGEST MISTAKE I MADE WAS WAITING TO INVEST IN RENTAL PROPERTIES

I didn't buy my first rental property until December of 2010 even though I had been around real estate my entire life. I had always wanted to invest in real estate, but I never had a definite plan for how to do it. I thought once I start making a lot of money I will be able to save more and buy some rental properties. Once I created my plan for investing, my savings started to grow, I started to spend more time researching the market and pretty soon I had my first property!

I will admit I had pretty good timing for starting to buy rental properties. Prices were low in 2010 and I got a great deal on my first rental property. If I would have started investing earlier in my career, I would have paid a lot more for a property. However, If I would have bought properties below market value with great cash flow I would still be in great shape. The sooner you buy investment properties, the sooner you start paying down mortgages and making money.

THE FOURTH BIGGEST MISTAKE I MADE WAS NOT SETTING GOALS

When I started out in real estate I never made goals, because I told myself I was smart enough and good enough that I didn't need goals. The truth is I was probably scared that I would not reach my goals and I would be a failure. This is a horrible attitude to have and we should never feel bad about falling short of our goals. Goals will almost always make us accomplish more than if we had no goals and that is what is important.

Goals help create a plan and vision, which is what I was lacking when I started in the business. If I would have set goals for myself in the beginning I know I would have had much more success. Now I create goals for everything, like my plan to purchase 100 properties.

THE FIFTH BIGGEST MISTAKE WAS BUYING A HOUSE THAT I COULD NOT AFFORD

When I bought my first house, I could afford it according to my lender. I qualified with no problem and I could make my payments. However, I had bought a house with a payment that was almost 30% of my income. I had very little money left over after my house payment for savings. I ended up saving very little money until I started making much more money from REO. I feel homeowners need to spend much less than they can qualify for on a house. It is very difficult to save any money when you spend the maximum amount of money you can on a house payment. Saving money is a key to creating wealth and I waited way too long to save anything.

CONCLUSION

We should not be afraid to make mistakes, because that is the best way to learn. All the mistakes I listed may have caused me short-term problems, but in the long run they taught me great lessons and helped me get to where I am today. Anytime I make a mistake now I try to look at how that mistake will help me, not dwell how dumb it was.

24. How I Was Able to Buy a Lamborghini Thanks to My Attitude and Positive Thinking

Buying a Lamborghini has been a goal of mine since I was a little kid. Thanks to my real estate business and attitude changes, I was able to buy one May of 2014. It was actually delivered to me on Father's Day 2014. I wasn't planning on buying one at that time, but circumstances lined up and I could not pass this car up. My real estate business took off, the blog has took off, and this car was an awesome deal, as well as the perfect color.

Is it smart to buy a Lamborghini?

I will admit that being frugal is very popular right now and buying a Lamborghini is the farthest thing from being frugal. I want to be clear that one of the most important keys to wealth is saving money. Saving money gives you options like investing in rental properties or buying fix and flips, which allow you to make much more money. Saving money also allows you to be more flexible with your career or even start a business. If you never have any money saved, it is very hard to get ahead in life, no matter what you do. I would never have bought a car like this if I was not in a very good financial position and it was not extremely important to me.

I also don't believe in being cheap and skimping out on the things that make you happy. I have worked very hard to be in the position I am in now and I believe people need to do things that make them happy. Not everything that makes us happy takes money, but some things do. Do not refuse or be afraid to spend money on things that truly make you happy, especially after you have worked your butt off and earned it.

Many people will question how wise it is to buy a $100,000 car, but I think it was a great decision. Wanting this car motivated me every day and allowed to me to improve my business, take chances and be more successful. I am a car nut and buying a car like this may not motivate others like it has me. Pick something to motivate you that you really want and use it to motivate and push you farther.

HOW MAKING GOALS HELPED ME BUY A LAMBORGHINI

I also believe making big goals that motivate you, will make you more successful. Making big goals that are exciting and easily visualized, like buying a Lamborghini can really motivate you. Some might say making goals like providing for your family or retiring early are more important, but how easy is it to picture providing for your family or retiring early? Obviously these are important big picture goals, but these goals are very vague and it is difficult to picture them. If I say I want a 1999 blue Lamborghini Diablo that is specific and easy to picture!

I have had many other big goals and small goals including my plan to purchase 100 rental properties. Goals have helped me tremendously in making more money, buying more investments, saving money and improving my personal life. I am less stressed now than I have ever been and spend more time with my family than I ever have.

WHY DID I WANT TO BUY A LAMBORGHINI?

I have loved exotic cars since I was a young child. I had many car books, hot wheels and model cars that I always played with. I loved Ferrari's, Lamborghini's, Maserati's, Aston Martin's and many more makes of cars. Over the years the Lamborghini's grew on me more and more. They were extremely rare, very fast, very unique and basically outrageous automobiles.

I always wanted a Lamborghini and I believed I would have one when I was a kid. When I got into the real world everyone tells you to do your job, make a decent living, save for retirement and you'll be happy. It was hammered into my head to not want expensive cars or houses, because the chances were I would never have those things. After a few years of taking the traditional route, I decided I wanted more.

I decided in my late 20's I could have an exotic car and I could do it in the next decade or two. I started setting goals, making plans and making my future. I became a REO agent, my real estate career took off and I started being able to save a lot of money. I started investing in rental properties, doing more fix and flips, I started Invest Four More and bought the real estate business from my father.

Suddenly I was reaching goals quicker than I ever thought possible. I had to constantly change and create more aggressive goals. I believe in very aggressive goals, because they will push you harder than easy goals. If you achieve all your goals quickly, you may not be motivated to keep working hard. If you don't reach your goals, it is not a big deal because you will better off having chased that huge goal than not having goals or reaching an easy goal. After all of this change and success, I decided to make a huge goal to buy a Diablo in 2014.

WHY DID I WANT TO BUY A LAMBORGHINI DIABLO?

My dream car when I was a child was a Lamborghini Countach. The Countach was an outrageous, rear engined V-12, sports car that was introduced in the early 1970's. The Countach was like nothing else on the road in the 70's, 80's or even now.

I did a lot of research on the Countach and found it was very small, not easy to drive, not very reliable and more of a show car than a driving car. I like to drive my cars, not look at them in the garage. At a conference in Dallas at the end of 2013, I stopped at Lamborghini of Dallas because they had a Diablo. I had searched for a dealership or someone with a Countach, but could not find one anywhere in the country.

The Diablo was an awesome car and I liked it much more than newer Lamborghini Models; the Gallardo and Murcialago. The Aventador is the newest model; a 700 horsepower work of art, but they are $450,000 to $550,000. The best part about the Diablo was I fit! Although my shoe would not fit between the brake pedal and sidewall to touch the gas pedal, I had plenty of leg room and head room. I figured I could figure out the pedal problem later.

After seeing the Diablo and learning about the Countach, my new goal was to buy a Diablo. The Diablo is still a rear engined V-12 with outrageous styling, 530 horsepower and it was the first production car to go 200 MPH (unless you count the Ferrari F40, which was more of a race car). They built a little over 2,000 Diablos from 1991 to 2001. The Diablos are much rarer than the newer model Lamborghini's and in my opinion better looking and more exotic.

WHAT ARE THE COSTS ASSOCIATED WITH OWNING A LAMBORGHINI DIABLO?

You have to do a lot of homework before buying a car like this. I found a local dealership that will work on the Diablo as well as Lamborghini of Denver, which is about 45 miles from me. The car needs an oil change every 7,500 miles, which is about $750 (some Ferrari's require engine out oil changes which are much more expensive). The cars need a major service every 15,000 miles which is about $2,500 to $3,000. These costs are from the local shop, not Lamborghini of Denver which would be more expensive.

Insurance for the car through my regular insurance company was only $800 a year! There are some other items that break like clutches ($5,000 +) and parts will wear out on a 15 to 25-year-old car. Before I bought this car I had everything repaired that was worn. However, I still know there will be many more costs associated with this car than a normal automobile.

WHAT KIND OF DIABLO DID I BUY?

My Lamborghini Diablo (boy it feels good saying that) is a 1999 VT Alpine edition with a 5 speed manual transmission. They made 12 Alpine edition Diablos, which had an upgraded stereo from Alpine as well as more carbon fiber than the regular Diablo. The Alpine edition is rare, but doesn't add much value since there are no performance upgrades.

The car is finished in Monterey Blue with snow corn white interior. I love this color and that is one reason I bought this car. I wanted a blue Diablo with a light or white interior. The interior is not actually white, but more of a tan color. There are no numbers on how many Diablos were painted Monterey Blue, but I would guess under 20 from what I have read.

The year this car was built is also important, because Audi bought Lamborghini in 1998 and from that point forward they became much more reliable cars. Lamborghini was actually owned by Chrysler in the late 1980's when the Diablo was developed. In 1999 and 2001 (they didn't make any in 2000) the Diablos became more reliable, more refined and more comfortable. I knew I wanted a 1999 or 2001 Diablo, which also had a new interior that was much more modern than the earlier cars.

The car is a VT, which stands for vicious traction and means it is all wheel drive. Most people don't realize most Lamborghini's are all wheel drive, although some are made with rear wheel drive to make them lighter and faster. The car has a 5 speed manual transmission, which was the only option. Newer Lamborghini's are more likely to have an E gear (automatic transmission with paddle shifter) than a true manual transmission with a clutch. They do not even make Lamborghini's or Ferrari's with a manual transmission now. There was simply no demand from new buyers for what I feel is one of the best parts of my Lamborghini, the gated manual transmission.

My particular Diablo has 21,000 miles, looked to be in great shape and was for sale at a dealership in Washington

State. Cats Exotics is the dealership and one of the best dealerships for Diablos and exotic cars in the country.

The owner is an exotic car lover who started a dealership. I had a pre purchase inspection done on the car and found a few times that needed repaired. Before I had the car shipped to me, the rear bushings were replaced, a door strut replaced and spark plus replaced ($50 apiece) as part of the deal. The inspection showed the compression in the engine was good and the rest of the car looked to be in great shape.

WHY DID I BUY THIS LAMBORGHINI DIABLO?

I was not planning on buying a Diablo this soon, but I thought I might be able to buy one at the end of 2014. I saw this car for sale early this year and I knew it was the perfect color. I kept an eye on It, and a couple of months ago I noticed it was scheduled to go to auction in June. If it went to auction I would not have a chance to inspect the car and I would be charged a 5 percent buyer's premium on top of my bid. There was no guarantee my bid would hit the reserve and I had to pay $100 just to register at the auction (Mecum). I knew my best chance to buy the car was to buy it from the dealer before the auction. I knew if someone else bought this car, my chances of finding a similar car this color or any blue color would be very low.

It may seem a little crazy, but I bought this car without seeing it in person. In fact I had never driven a Diablo before I bought this car. I put my trust in a dealership with an awesome reputation and a mechanic who used to work for Ferrari and Lamborghini.

HOW MUCH WAS THE LAMBORGHINI DIABLO?

The car was listed for $134,900 on the website for the dealer. I knew it was going to auction and the dealer would be motivated. He said he would sell it for $125,000 to me since it was going to auction. I tried to negotiate more, but there was no budging. After thinking about the car for weeks decided to move forward with the purchase. I had the inspection done

147

and a few items popped up that were worn, but didn't need replaced right away. As part of the deal I had the worn items fixed or replaced and the dealer sold the car for $126,000.

I actually bought the car in early May, but had to wait for a door strut to come from Italy and have the mechanic fix it, before the car was shipped. Shipping took another 10 days and the car arrived Father's Day!

I mentioned the Countach was a dream of mine and one reason the Diablo worked out better was the cost of a Countach. The Countach has seen its value increase 300 percent in the last four years! I believe the Diablo is at its low value now and will start to increase as well. Not that I bought the car as an investment, but it will be nice to see it go up in value instead of down like most cars. The car was about $300,000 new in 1999. (A couple of years later this car is now worth well over $200,000!)

HOW DID REAL ESTATE HELP ME BUY THE DIABLO?

My real estate career took off as soon as I started setting goals and planning my future. I did not do so well in the beginning, when I thought everything would come to me and I would not have to work hard to make a lot of money. With real estate I was able to start small, build up my business, hire assistants, then start hiring agents and now I have a team of ten people. I also have 10 rental properties with an 11th under contract (10 when I bought the car). The real estate team does great, although I am constantly trying to increase production. I make over $50,000 a year from my rental properties in cash flow. I flip from 10 to 15 homes a year, which bring in about $30,000 in profit each. I have Invest Four More, which brings in a decent income as well. One of my rewards to myself was to start looking seriously at Diablos when Invest Four More made enough money to cover the monthly payment and costs of the

Diablo. Thank you to everyone who visits the site and helped make this happen!

MY FUTURE PLANS FOR THE DIABLO

You have to see this car in person to appreciate it. It is lower and wider than almost any car you will ever see. I own a 1986 Porsche 928, which is very wide and low; the Diablo is 8 inches shorter and wider than the 928. There are people taking pictures of it every time I drive it, and one woman stopped in the middle of traffic at a green light to take a picture of it! I have to watch out for people swerving and not paying attention while they take their pictures.

The car obviously attracts a lot of attention and I am working on ways to use that to my advantage. I am working on a flyer that I can put on the dash while it is parked with information on me and our team. I am also looking into license plate frames with our team number on it and a few other options. I will not wrap the car with advertisements. Every time I stop anywhere multiple people come to talk to me. Every good real estate agent looks for reasons to talk to as many people as they can and with the Diablo everyone comes to me. I have a feeling the car will more than pay for itself.

NEW GOALS FOR THE FUTURE NOW THAT I BOUGHT THE DIABLO?

My wife and kids absolutely love the car. Every time I drive it, my three-year old twins come running out of the house to watch me drive away laughing hysterically (the car is very loud). My wife asked me what I am going to do now that I achieved this goal, how will I motivate myself? I showed her my phone which already has a picture of a 1970 Lamborghini Muira on the home screen. I had a picture of a Blue Lamborghini Diablo on my home screen for months before I bought the Diablo. The Muira is the most beautiful car every built in my opinion and about 8 times as expensive as the

Diablo. That will give me something to shoot for! I still love the looks of the Countach as well...

CONCLUSION

Don't be afraid to have big goals or want nice things. Those goals and things will help motivate you to make more money, be happier and even be a better person. Visualizing every day how awesome it would be to drive my Lamborghini Diablo helped me be more successful and make more money.

25. HOW I WAS ABLE TO BUY MY DREAM HOME MUCH SOONER THAN I EVER THOUGHT

This is a story about how we were able to buy our dream home almost three years ago. This was when I first was getting heavily into personal improvement and things were happening very quickly. I wanted to leave this story mostly intact from when I first wrote it, to show my mindset at the time.

This month we bought our dream home. The house is over 6,000 square feet, has a half acre lot, a five car garage and is awesome. I never would have thought I would have a house like this so quickly in life (34 years old). Real estate has helped me become very successful and a change in attitude has helped me make tremendous strides in life.

Through this entire process of buying a house and selling our old house, I have been very tired and sore, but relatively stress free. A huge reason I have been stress free, is at the beginning of 2013 I really got into personal improvement. I have always thought of myself as a relatively positive person, but I learned that the secret to being ultra-successful is taking your attitude to a new positive level. In the past 6 to 8 months I have read many books, listened to many books on CD and enrolled in a personal coaching program through Jack Canfield coaching. I think the biggest thing I have taken away from all of this, is to stop worrying and relax. The positive thinking has taught me that I can get what I want if I really go after it and not to stress about things.

WHAT MADE US THINK ABOUT MOVING?

My wife and I had thrown around the idea of building a loft in our old house for months, but had very little success figuring out how to make it work. The home we just moved out of is a ranch home, with a basement and has very steep pitched roof. I have been in the attic a few times (after climbing a ladder about 12 feet to the access in our garage), and there is tons of space in the attic. There is space for a 12 x 16 room with 10 foot ceilings and twice that much space with at least 8 foot ceilings. The peak of our attic is at least 16 feet high, and I thought for sure this was a great plan that would make our house awesome. The plan was to finish one big room, and connect it to our vaulted living room so that the loft would overlook the living room below. We would stack stairs on top of our current stairs and add a patio off the loft that would be high enough for a great view of the mountains over our neighbor's house.

We contacted a contractor and he was very positive about putting a loft in the attic, but warned us it could cost quite a bit. We were prepared for the cost if it was under $50,000 and decided to have an architect he knew, come look at the house. The architect came a couple of weeks later and he was also positive about our prospects for finishing the attic. He said he needed to talk to a structural engineer and would get back to us. A few weeks passed with no word from anyone and we were getting impatient. We asked our contractor, and he said he finally got a hold of the architect and he said he couldn't do it, it was too much work. I tried calling the architect to get more details and he never called me back.

We did not give up, I thought it was my destiny to have a loft in this house and I was going to make it happen! I called another contractor and another architect. The contractor told me to buy a new house with a loft, because the hassle wasn't worth it. The architect said, he would be happy to look at it and then disappeared. I still did not give up, this time I asked around for a structural engineer who I could talk to about the loft project. I kept hearing the same name pop up so I gave him a call. He sounded pessimistic from the beginning and said he was super busy with work. I gave him a call a couple of weeks later and convinced him to look at our house. He came over, saw the engineered trusses and said he could make it work, if he had the original drawings for the house.

The biggest issue from the beginning was the engineered trusses that cross throughout the attic. The engineer said they would all have to be rebuilt and engineered to make the space needed. The only way he would even consider the project was if I had the building plans. I went on a mission, I tracked down the builder (it was built in 2005) in Wyoming through LinkedIn. The builder responded and said yes he probably had the plans in his storage unit, he would look for them in the next couple of days. I never heard from him, so I asked again with the same response. This went on for months, so I offered him $100 for the plans if he could find them. He never responded and disappeared. I had checked with the city and the company that built the trusses, but neither one kept the plans.

I was starting to doubt that positive thinking and persistence was going to get me this loft. My coach had suggested I try offering the builder $300 for the plans to entice him to dig through his storage unit. I was thinking about it, but had to go to a real estate conference and decided to wait until after the conference to pursue anything else.

A SURPRISE AT THE CONFERENCE FROM MY WIFE

At the conference I remember sitting down talking to a friend, when I received a text from my wife. The text said something like "I found the perfect house!" She sent a link to the house, which seemed very nice, but was much more than we had ever thought about spending. During the last couple of months of trying to make the loft work, we had started to casually look for houses. We had looked at a couple and kept our eyes open, but were not thinking of moving unless we found an awesome deal on an amazing house.

The thing that really caught my eye about this house, was it had a five car garage. I have three cars, my wife has one and we have a lot of other junk in our garage as well. I currently keep one car at my sister's garage and I was seriously thinking about buying a shop or warehouse where I could put my car and all our extra junk (that junk consists of good deals she finds on materials for our fix and flips and rentals). I had a really hard time finding any shop space for rent or for sale, which was in my price range. I even went so far as to mail out 50 letters to every owner in a complex I liked, to see if anyone wanted to sell. I got one response, from someone who wanted way too much money on one of the worst units in the complex. The search for a commercial shop space was going about as well as the loft.

WHAT WAS THE HOUSE LIKE THAT MY WIFE SENT ME AT THE CONFERENCE?

Besides having a five car garage, the house has an awesome loft that overlooks the 2 story tall living room. The house has a view of open space, trees, a greenhouse and lake that are all part of a massive estate that recently sold for 3 million dollars (in our area that is a lot of money for any real estate). There are great views of the mountains from the upstairs and the home is on a half-acre lot. It has a finished walkout basement, pond with a waterfall, fenced yard, awesome kitchen, awesome master suite and a lot of space.

When I got back from my conference we saw the home
in person and my wife (Jeni) fell in love with it. I liked it, but I
was not so sure I liked it enough to pay what they were asking.
I did some research on comparable homes, since I had never
paid much attention to this price range. I found there were not
many comparable homes on the market. This house had more
features and fit us better than any similarly priced home
or even more expensive homes.

As a Realtor and house lover, I like to look at large homes. In
my experience builders ten to chop up the floor plan, add
useless features and ruin the floor plans of large homes. This
house was not like that at all, it had a large living room open to
the kitchen and breakfast nook. The builder had actually used
the space to make larger functional rooms that I would actually
use! The more I thought about it, the more I liked this house,
especially since the comparable houses did not have 5 car
garages, did not have a lake view, and did not have anywhere
close to as nice of a floor plan.

HOW MUCH DID WE OFFER ON THE HOUSE?

We decided to make an offer on the home, after I came to the
realization that a house like this does not come on the market
often, and I may never find one that fits us this well. I wrote an
article on my blog about how much people can really afford to

spend on a house and came to find out we could afford this house. I calculated this home cost close to a million dollars to build, with all the high-tech features. The asking price was $600,000 and we offered $520,000 with the sellers paying $5,000 in closing costs. Along with the offer, my wife wrote the sellers a letter, explaining how the house was perfect for us. How the loft would allow her to sew, while she watched our twins play and added many other sweet things in the letter.

We received a response the next day that they had received another offer on the home. The Realtor said our offer was much lower than the other offer, but the sellers loved Jeni's letter and they were thinking it over. I decided I did not want to miss out on this house, we decided to raise our offer significantly. We raised our offer to $555,000 and I waved my commission, basically making our offer $571,650, with the sellers paying $5,000 in closing costs. The home also has a theatre room and two laundry rooms, so we asked for all the theatre equipment, seating and one washer and dryer to be included with our offer.

We patiently waited, hoping that our offer was good enough, even though it was still below asking price. The sellers had just bought the home 6 months earlier, but had to move because they have a special needs child, who did not do well in the local school system. They had bought the home for $560,000 and we thought our offer was pretty fair based on their purchase price. A day later I received a call from the listing agent and he told me they will accept $555,000 without the inclusions or $560,000 with the inclusions. I told them we will do it for $560,000 with the inclusions and we had a deal!

We set our closing out 7 weeks because the sellers were going to be out-of-town and we had to figure out how we were going to make all this work. Our current house was not near show condition and I had not even thought about selling it yet. Luckily we were able to buy the new house without selling the current house, but I didn't want to pay two mortgage any longer than I had too.

INSPECTION, APPRAISAL, CLOSING ON THE NEW HOUSE

Everything with the new house went fairly smooth. We did our inspection and found many minor problems, but nothing huge. We only asked for a window seal to be fixed which, was about two hundred dollars. The appraisal came in at $575,000, which was a surprise since appraisers rarely come in higher than contract price. My lender said we were all set and we just had to wait for closing. I ended up doing a 7 year ARM with my portfolio lender at 3.375 percent.

HOW BUYING THIS HOUSE RELATES TO POSITIVE THINKING

I don't think there is any way I would have bought this house without my attitude change. I would have never considered this house before, thinking it was too much money. With my new positive attitude came the idea to do as many exciting things as possible in my life. Buying this house is definitely exciting and makes me even more positive and happy thinking about it.

The weirdest thing about the entire situation, is one of my tasks for my coaching program. I was asked to write story that explained how my ideal life would be in ten years. I was to be as detailed as possible and include information on my family, house, cars, job, income and what I do in my free time and for work (if anything). I wrote out a story that described my life and I described the house I wanted to live in. Here is how I described my ideal house in ten years.

"Jeni and I have moved from our current house, we loved it especially after the loft was built, but decided to build our dream house. The house is still in town, but has a .5 acre lot. Our house has 6,000 square feet with a walk out basement, loft, fantastic master suite and a huge kitchen. The great part about the property is the massive 15 car garage/shop."

I recorded my ten-year dream story and listened to it at least once a day for a month or two. I had stopped listening to that story right before we made the offer on the house since I had made many other recordings that I listened to instead. I have recordings for my goals, affirmations and one year dream story. I happened to listen to my ten-year dream story a few weeks after we had the house under contract and could not believe how similar the house we had under contract was to my description. The only real difference was the 15 car shop, but a 5 car garage is pretty rare around here and there is room on the lot to build a shop.

The kitchen and master suite are definitely fantastic in this house. The master bedroom is 19 x 19, has an infinity overflow tub with the faucet coming out of the ceiling and LED lights in the tub. The master closet is 10 x 12 with an island and attached laundry room. The shower is huge with four shower heads.

The kitchen is 19 x 19 with slab granite, copper hood, gas range, three dishwashers, double oven, two beverage coolers, side by side built-in fridge with four drawer freezers, 7 x 6 island and 12 foot long breakfast bar.

The theatre room is another fantastic feature. It has six electronic theatre seats, a Polk audio sound system, projector, black walls with movie theatre curtains and tiered seats.

Don't be afraid to ask for what you want

A lot of the books and CDs I listen too, have a common point. You have to continually tell your subconscious what you want and your subconscious will do it's best to deliver it to you. Recording my dream story, affirmations and goals is all supposed to help my subconscious understand what I want and it seems to be working!

The less you worry about things, the less stress you will have

The most important thing I have gotten out of my coaching is letting go of stress and worry. One of the big ones for me was constantly worrying and thinking about my business and money. When I became successful I started to thinking to myself don't screw this up. I constantly worried about losing business or what would happen if I lost a source of income and worried about how much we spent on everything.

I have learned this is a really horrible way to think. For one thing, your subconscious hears all these negative thoughts and worries towards money. That naturally makes your subconscious think you want to lose your money, since your subconscious can't tell the difference between a negative and a positive. That is why being positive all the time is so important, if your happy and positive then your subconscious does it's best to keep you that way. At the same time when you think about things you like and make you happy, your subconscious tries to help you get those things. If you think about things you don't like and don't want, your subconscious also tries to help you get those things as well.

My coaching helped me realize worrying about money does no good, in fact worrying about anything does not good. I can't change the past and I can't predict the future. All I can do is try my best in life and have faith things will work out. Most of our fear and worry is based on future events that our mind has convinced us will happen. Usually those events never happen and all the worry did nothing, but cause us stress. It may seem hard to believe, but this new philosophy has almost eliminated worry and stress in my life. Throughout this entire house buying process, I knew things would work out for the best and I think they have.

BUT DID I PUT MYSELF IN A BAD FINANCIAL POSITION THINKING THIS WAY?

Because I have a lot of equity in my old house, we are breaking even with the down payment for the new house and the proceeds from the old house. If we would have been able to make the loft work in the old house, it would have cost us more money than buying a new house. If we would have bought a commercial shop, it would have cost us more money than buying a new house. By buying a new house we were able to solve the loft issue, the shop issue and we got an amazing new house. Those may all be coincidences, but what makes it even more unlikely is how the sale of our house worked out. My good friend bought it, who is moving from out of town to work with me. I did not have to market my old house, make any repairs and it closed right away!

While we did buy a much more expensive home that has a higher house payment, I believe it was a good financial decision.

- We put less cash into the home than we would have building a loft or buying a shop.
- If we had built a loft, we would not have recouped the investment when we sold the house.
- Having a five car garage allowed me to set and achieve the goal of buying a Lamborghini.
- I realized I could afford the new payment when I ran the numbers and still have plenty of money to invest.
- We are on a street that is sager for our kids.
- We got a great deal on the home.

I do not think the dream story and making a goal to buy this house, magically made it appear. However, it put the idea in my head and subconscious. I did not even find the house, my wife did! She happened to find it, because she took a wrong turn on a new road that happened to go right past this home. After living in the home for three years, it has made us all very happy and been a great decision. The home has increased in value, which allowed me to take out a line of credit for more investing.

26.   HOW DO MOST MILLIONAIRES MAKE THEIR MONEY?

Making one million dollars a year is not as impressive as it was in the past thanks to inflation. However, it is still a goal for many people and many people consider millionaires to be "rich". To qualify as a millionaire you simply have to have one million dollars in net worth, which is not as rare as it used to be. There are many studies on wealth, but from what I could research about 6 percent of United States households are considered millionaires. It is interesting to see to more and more people becoming millionaires thanks to inflation and also to a strong economy. The question I am curious about is how do people become millionaires? Is it through inheritance, investment, saving, business, real estate or a combination of many sources? While it is great to use the techniques I talk about in this book to become more successful. You also have to do your homework when deciding how to become successful in life. Learning from those who have already succeeded in life is a great way to choose a path.

I am considered a millionaire and I made my money almost entirely through being an agent, by flipping houses and by owning rental properties. While selling houses as a real estate agent and flipping houses makes a lot of money, owning rental properties has increased my net worth the most. It is great to make a lot of money, but you need to make sure you have something to show for it by saving and investing.

HOW DO MOST PEOPLE BECOME BILLIONAIRES?

I have been researching how most people became millionaires for a very long time. I cannot find a survey or survey results that gives a straight answer! I can find how most billionaires made their money and the statistics are listed below for the US and the world.

Top 10 Industries Producing U.S. Billionaires

1. Investments: 100

2. Technology: 51

3. Media: 37

4. Energy: 35

5. Food and Beverage: 31

5. Service: 31

7. Fashion and Retail: 28

8. Real Estate: 27

9. Manufacturing: 18

10. Sports: 15

Global Top 10 Industries Producing Billionaires

1. Investments: 143

2. Fashion & Retail: 123

3. Real Estate: 102

4. Diversified: 97

5. Technology: 90

6. Manufacturing: 85

7. Energy: 78

8. Finance: 77

9. Food & Beverage: 69

10. Media: 64

While it is interesting to see how most people became billionaires, the average person does not have a very good chance of becoming a billionaire or may not even want to be a billionaire. I have found a couple of articles that claim 80 percent of millionaires made their money with real estate and some that say as many as 90 percent. However I can't find sources for the studies or where this information came from. However, it does not surprise me that most people become millionaires because of real estate.

WHY DOES REAL ESTATE PRODUCE SO MANY MILLIONAIRES?

Many people will argue that stocks or mutual funds are a much better investment than real estate, because the average gain of the stock market is higher than the average gain of housing prices over the last 100 years. However, when you invest in real estate or even buy a house to live in, the wealth you are gaining is not as simple as the increase in value of the home.

- **Leverage**: Most people get a loan when they buy a house. Getting a loan increases your returns if housing prices increase. If you buy a house for $100,000 and it increases in value to $120,000, which is a 20 percent increase in value. But if you only put $10,000 down on the property, then you actually made a 200 percent increase on your investment.
- **Buy below market**: When I buy houses I do not pay retail value, I want a great deal and you can do that with real estate. Many houses can be bought for less than they are worth if the seller is motivated, the home needs repairs or for many other reasons. On my rental properties and fix and flips I usually pay at least 20 percent below market value. As soon I buy the house I increase my net worth by the discount I got on the property.
- **Cash flow**: Owning rental properties is not all about the value of the home increasing. In fact I pay more attention to the cash flow my properties make me, not appreciation. My rental properties make me about

$500 a month, which is $8,000 a year. That is not a ton of money, but when you buy multiple properties that money begins to add up. I own 16 rentals at the moment and I am looking to own at least 100.

- **Equity pay down:** When you use leverage to buy rental properties you are paying down the balance of the loan every month. Depending on the type of loan you get, you could pay off the house in 30 years, 15 years or sooner if you want to pay off the loan early.
- **Tax advantages**: Real estate has awesome tax advantages for your personal house and for investment properties. In some cases you can make money on cash flow every month and pay no taxes thanks to depreciation. You can also use a 1031 exchange to defer taxes on sales.

Buying one rental property and holding it for 30 years may not make you a millionaire. Actually it most likely would make you a millionaire thanks to inflation, but being a millionaire in 30 years will not be the same as being a millionaire today. If you can buy multiple properties over time that are great deals you can become a millionaire rather quickly. You don't even have to have a lot of money to start with.

WHAT OTHER WAYS CAN REAL ESTATE MAKE YOU A MILLIONAIRE?

We just discussed how rental properties can make you a millionaire, but there are many other ways to make a lot of money with real estate.

- **Development**: Probably the way to make the most money the fastest in real estate is by developing land into residential or commercial projects. This technique also extremely risky and takes a lot of money and experience. I know a couple of real estate developers in my area who are worth close to or over 100 million and many of the billionaires who used real estate are developers.

166

- **Building homes**: Building goes hand in hand with developing and is another way to make a lot of money, but can be very risky if the markets turn.
- **Owning raw land**: Raw land can be developed, but it also can make you rich without development. Many farmers have become millionaires because they owned large plots of land close to developing areas. The closer the towns get to their land the more it is worth. Mineral rights can also be extremely valuable if oil, natural gas or other resources are found on your land.

WHAT OTHER FACTORS CONTRIBUTE TO BECOMING A MILLIONAIRE?

If you want to be rich, you can't go out and buy a few houses and assume they will make you rich. You have to educate yourself, made a plan and have the right attitude. This article has some very cool data on how rich think differently than the poor. Here are some highlights from a survey that defines rich people as those with an annual income of $160,000 or more and a liquid net worth of $3.2 million or more, and poor people as those with an annual income of $35,000 or less and a liquid net worth of $5,000 or less.

1. "Daily habits are critical to financial success in life."
Rich people who agree: 52%
Poor people who agree: 3%

2. "The American dream is no longer possible."
Rich people who agree: 2%
Poor people who agree: 87%

3. "Relationships are critical to financial success."
Rich people who agree: 88%
Poor people who agree: 17%

4. "I love meeting new people."

Rich people who agree: 68%
Poor people who agree: 11%

5. "Saving money is critical to financial success."
Rich people who agree: 88%
Poor people who agree: 52%

6. "I believe in fate."
Rich people who agree: 10%
Poor people who agree: 90%

7. "Creativity is critical to financial success."
Rich people who agree: 75%
Poor people who agree: 11%

8. "I like (or liked) what I do for a living."
Rich people who agree: 85%
Poor people who agree: 2%

9. "Good health is critical to financial success."
Rich people who agree: 85%
Poor people who agree: 13%

10. "I've taken a risk in search of wealth."
Rich people who agree: 63%
Poor people who agree: 6%

You don't have to use real estate to become a millionaire, but you do have to have the right outlook and attitude. These results show some very consistent and clear data regarding why rich people make more money. They are willing to take chances, they are willing to get out of their comfort zone by meeting new people, they love what they do for a living, they save their money and they believe that their actions are what will make them successful.

Many people feel the wealthy had an unfair advantage growing up and that is why they became successful. Statistics show that 80 percent or more of the wealthy were self-made. Studies also show that people who are first generation Americans are more likely to become millionaires than those that have lived in the country for multiple generations. Theories suggest people who live here for multiple generations gain habits of spending too much money, which makes it hard to ever become rich no matter how much money you make. People who come from other countries also want to take full advantage of the opportunities the US provides compared to where they came from.

WHAT STEPS CAN YOU TAKE RIGHT NOW TO BECOME A MILLIONAIRE?

You don't have to use real estate to become rich, but I feel it is one of the easier ways to make a lot of money. Whether you choose real estate or another avenue to make your money doing these things will make the journey easier.

- **Do something that you like doing**. If you hate your job and can't wait until you can go home every day, it is very unlikely you will give the extra effort it takes to get ahead.
- **Save Money**: Yes I bought a Lamborghini, but I saved money for many years before buying it. I also bought the car partially as an investment and it has increased on value this last year.
- **Make goals and plan your life:** Most people drift through life hoping success will find them somehow. It doesn't work that way, you have to find success and make it happen. Start by writing out how you want your life to be in the future and then make goals and plans that will help you make it a reality.
- **Start your own businesses**: 75 percent of millionaires are self-employed even though only 20 percent of the work force is self-employed.
- **Don't be afraid to learn from those before you**: Whatever you do, there has been someone else who has tried it before. Most likely there are people who have written about it or have created products to help those who want to get started. Don't try to do everything on your own, because it will take longer and your chances of success will be less.

- **Associate with people who believe in you**: If you are constantly around negative people who tell you that you can't succeed you probably won't succeed. Choose friends and associates wisely who are supportive and encouraging.

Becoming rich is not easy. Many people who inherit wealth or have money come easily to them lose it. If you want to get ahead of the game and live an awesome life you have to do what most people aren't willing to do. Otherwise we would all be rich! Whether you choose real estate or another avenue to make your riches, make sure you choose the path and you do whatever falls in your lap because it is the easiest route. Most people will won't follow through with their plans or intentions when things get tough, don't be most people.

27.   WHAT IS THE EASIEST WAY TO START A BUSINESS?

Many people think of starting a business as a very difficult and involved process. You have to think of a brilliant idea, and figure how to implement that idea before anyone else does. You must have a ton of capital to get the business started and it might take years and years for the business to make money. In reality starting a successful business does not require a brilliant idea, a ton of money or many years of time. Although, having a brilliant idea, time, and money, does not hurt.

With today's technology it is easier than ever to start a business. There are online businesses that make millions of dollars a year and have no physical product or store. The ways to make money with a business are unlimited, but too many people think the process is much harder than it is. A brilliant idea is not needed to start a business, because there is often room for more than one company in a given niche. Many times competitors are not doing things as well as they should and you can be successful by taking old ideas and implementing them better. My specialty is real estate as you know. There are thousands of real estate investors and millions of real estate agents. Yet, people make millions in real estate every day and I feel it is one of the easiest businesses to start.

WHAT IS A SUCCESSFUL BUSINESS?

I think too many people get caught up with what they envision a business as. They think of physical stores, restaurants, law firms, dentists etc. But there are many businesses that can be started fairly cheaply and quickly. You don't have to have a brilliant idea to have an awesome business. Owning rental properties, flipping houses or being a real estate agent can all be successful businesses. To me a successful business is not just about how much money you make, but how much time you spend working and if the business can run without you.

The idea of success will also vary based on what someone's goals are. $3,000 a month in passive income might be considered success to one person, while making $500,000 a year in profit might be considered success to someone else. I think too many business owners get caught up doing all the work in their business and cannot take a vacation or time off because things will fall apart. Whether your goals is $500 a month in extra income or $100,000 a month income, you have to think about how much time it takes you to work in your business and if you can take a vacation without the business falling apart.

A successful business should be able to run by itself for at least a short period of time. If you have to work all the time then you are working a job, not running a business. If you are making $100,000 a month you may be able to justify the work you put into the business for the tremendous rewards.
However, couldn't you also hire someone to do more of the work you are doing? You would make a little less money, but have less stress and more time. When you start your business make sure you remember why you started and don't get stuck doing a job every day.

WHY DON'T YOU NEED A BRILLIANT IDEA TO START A BUSINESS?

I think too many people get caught up in thinking of an idea before they start a business. Most never start a business because they never come up with that fool-proof idea that makes them millions. You don't have to be an awesome inventor or have an awesome idea to be a success. In fact, many of the people who invented some of our most used items today or had brilliant ideas for businesses did not make much money from those ideas. It was not the person or company with the brilliant idea that made the money, it was the person or company that figured out how to monetize that idea by marketing better, making the idea better or simply running their business smarter.

Instead of wasting years trying to think of a brilliant idea. Start a business that has an easy barrier to entry, you enjoy and you are knowledgeable about. Even if you do come up with a brilliant idea for a product, do you know how to produce it, market it and where are you going to get the capital to bring it into reality? The simpler the business the better and the easier it is to get started.

WHY IS ARE REAL ESTATE BUSINESSES EASY TO START AND MAKE SUCCESSFUL?

I am obviously biased, because I have multiple real estate businesses. However, I have a lot of experience starting businesses and real estate businesses are pretty simple to start and can be very profitable. Below is a list of real estate businesses that can be started easily and make a lot of money.

- **Rental properties**: Buying a rental property is an awesome business. Many people do not think of owning a home as a business, but rentals, produce income, have relatively stable value and are easy to finance.
- **Flipping houses**: Buying flips is harder than buying rentals, but it can still be a great business model. Buy low, repair and sell high is the simple formula to make money flipping.
- **Real estate agents:** Most people consider being an agent a job, but it is a business. Most agents are self-employed and should think of themselves as a business. It is also very easy to start a team, who can sell houses and make the head agent money with little work.

WHY ARE RENTAL PROPERTIES SUCH A GREAT BUSINESS MODEL?

Buying rental properties probably won't make you a millionaire overnight. This is not a get rich quick business, but it is a very profitable business and passive business if set up right. The trick to having a successful rental property business is buying properties below market value, with great cash flow, that produce great cash-on-cash returns. I own 16 rentals and bring in about $8,000 a month in profit after all expenses and paying a property manager.

The really nice part about rental properties is you can hire a property manager who will do almost all of the work for you. Turn-key rentals can be even more passive than regular rental properties and still produce great returns. Buying rentals can be expensive since most investors will have to put at least 20 percent down. However, there are many options to buy rentals with less out-of-pocket cash. They can also be hard to finance if you have multiple properties, but they are still easier to finance than most businesses.

The really nice thing about rental properties, is they are a valuable asset even if the business makes no money. If you start a business that fails and makes no money, you probably will have nothing to show for you work. Not many people want to buy a business that loses money. But rental properties have dual purposes, especially if you invest in single family homes. You might buy the wrong property that can't cash flow, because your loan was too expensive or the market is not conducive to cash flow. You can still sell that property to an owner occupant, who doesn't care what it rents for.

WHY IS FLIPPING AN EASY BUSINESS TO START?

Flipping houses is another great business that can be started fairly easily. You don't have to quit your job to flip a house and you don't have to spend all your time working on the business. The secret to flipping houses is buying them cheap enough to make money after accounting for all costs. Most of your time in this business should be spend finding deals, finding the right contractors and making sure those contractors do a good job.

I personally love flipping houses, but once you flip a house you will not make any more money, unless you find another house to flip. I like to take much of my flipping profits and buy rentals that will produce ongoing income. It can be tough to finance flips, but usually it is easier than funding another type of business. You also have a hard asset that will be valuable even if you screw up and lose money on the flip.

Flipping houses is a less passive business than owning rental properties, but it can be set up so the business owner is not working all the time. I have contractors that do all the work, I have a rehab manager who manages those contractors and I have other team members who allow me to focus on buying great deals.

WHY IS BECOMING A REAL ESTATE AGENT A GREAT BUSINESS TO GET INTO?

Being a real estate agent is running a business. Many agents do not think of it as a business but real estate agents are self-employed and you can run a team just like a business. On my team I have 6 licensed agents, a team manager, a contract manager and a couple of part-time assistants as well. My real estate team does an awesome job of running itself with minimal effort from me. I still conduct training and come up with new marketing ideas, but I can go on vacation with no worries and my team will be just fine.

Even if an agent does not have a team, they should act like a business. You should have a marketing budget, keep track of expenses, and try to build your business so it can run without you. That might mean hiring an assistant or partnering up with other agents who can help with your business when you can't be there. Being a real estate agent may be the easiest business to start in real estate, because you don't need good credit or a lot of cash to buy a house. You need to get your real estate license and join a brokerage to be an agent.

The problem with being a real estate agent is that most agents do not have plans, goals and the training needed to succeed. They put the time in "at their job" and assume they will make money because they are working. A business owner and real estate agent you have to spend your time wisely and not just put your time in. You must do the right activities that make money and real estate agents can make a lot of money when they work smart.

CONCLUSION

Starting a business can be very scary. It takes money, time, hard work and a lot of planning to do things right. I think real estate is one of the best businesses to be in and can have some awesome rewards versus the risks involved. Even if real estate is not a business you want to be in, make sure you remember why you started a business in the first place. Whether it was for freedom, passive income or something else. Too many business owners get sucked into working in the business and creating another job for themselves.

28.   DO YOU NEED A DETAILED BUSINESS PLAN TO BE SUCCESSFUL?

Many people feel they have to come up with a brilliant idea before they can start a business. Or they must have a 300 page business plan in place, approved by ten people, before they can risk going out on their own. In my experience it is good to have a plan, an idea, and be prepared, but you don't have to have every contingency planned for. In fact, sometimes a mediocre plan and idea will work if you have the ability to see things through, work hard and be flexible when starting a business. Success is not about brilliant ideas and knowing how everything will work before you start. The world is full of brilliant ideas that never went anywhere and the best plans will have to be changed. Some of my businesses and best ideas were started on a lark with little planning, but I started! When I got started my path became clearer and I was able to change and adjust my plans based on what was working.

IS IT OKAY TO START A BUSINESS WITHOUT A DETAILED PLAN?

There is a great saying from T. Harv Eker and he may have gotten it from someone else.

"Ready fire aim"

Most people spend all their time aiming and preparing for their first shot to hit the bull's eye. Personally I know very few people who can hit a bull's eye on the first try. When you are spending time lining up your aim, you could be firing away. The first shot will tell you how far off you are and how to adjust your aim for the second shot. If the second shot isn't true, then adjust your aim for the third shot and so on. The truth is people rarely hit the target dead on with their first shot. It takes practice and trial by error to hit that target.

This metaphor is perfect for business and most anything you do in life. No matter how much you plan for something, the best way to get to where you want to be is to start moving. Take action and begin, then when you see some results and feedback on what you are doing you can adjust your course or continue dead ahead. It is rare that our original plans are what we end up with in the end.

HOW MUCH PLANNING DO YOU NEED WHEN YOU START A BUSINESS?

Even though it may seem really easy to fire at a target without aiming, there is still a lot of work involved. You have to decide what you are shooting with, what your target is, when you are going to shoot and where. You can't blindly set up any business and hope it will succeed with a few adjustments. You do have to have some sort of plan, idea and it helps if you are passionate about the business. It is hard to say exactly how much planning is needed for a certain business since a lot will depend on someone's situation.

If you are a single mom who is quitting her job and you have to support your kids, you will need to be more careful starting a business than someone who is retired and has all the money they need. Some businesses you may be able to start part-time while you keep your day job.

- You can be a real estate agent part-time, although it is tough and your schedule needs to be flexible.
- You can flip houses part-time, but I suggest not making all the repairs yourself.
- You can buy rentals part-time as well.
- You can start an online company part-time like a blog or small retailer.
- There are many other business that can be done part-time as well if they are set up correctly.

If you are quitting your job and putting everything you have into a business, you may need to have a detailed business plan and account for as many contingencies as you can. You also don't want to get stuck in analysis paralysis and never make the jump, because you don't have everything planned.

As you can see it is really hard to answer the question of how much planning you need. I will give some examples of how I started some of my businesses to show what I have done.

HOW DID I START A SUCCESSFUL REAL ESTATE BLOG?

It is hard to say exactly how many blogs there are, but it is estimated there are over 150 million! Very few of them will ever make money or be "successful". I knew this when I started Invest Four More back in 2013, but I still started it and here is how it happened:

I was at a conference in Dallas and was lucky enough to be on a panel on stage. This was my first time doing something like this and being a natural introvert it was incredibly scary and exciting at the same time. On the panel we were asked if we blogged and how it helped our real estate business. Not one of us said yes we have a blog and I had absolutely no inclination to start a blog. That was late January of 2013. Somehow in less than six weeks I had come up with the idea to start a blog and I wrote my first articles.

What's even funnier is how I came up with the idea for the blog. Justin my team manager had some help with the idea. But here is how the idea first evolved:

- Justin was still working at a large corporation as a senior level manager. We had both gotten on the positive thinking self-help kick. We were brainstorming ideas to start a new business.
- I was trying to think of what was missing in the world of real estate. At that time it was really hard for investors to get more than four loans. (It still is hard if you don't know where to look) I had a local lender that

would finance me, but I knew that was hard to find for many people. I decided I would start a national bank specializing in investment loans.

- I started researching how to start a bank, what the federal requirements were and I even found a website that detailed how I could start my own bank! The problem I faced was simple: it is incredibly hard to start a bank. I had no contacts, not a lot of money and no experience in banking.
- I spent a lot of time figuring out if I could really start a bank. I came to the conclusion that I could not or at least it was not worth the incredible effort it would take.
- I did not just give up. I still had knowledge of how to get loans and I knew there was a missing piece in the market place. Justin suggested I start a blog. So I did. I had no idea what I was doing, I hadn't written anything since college and I am not a techy person. I still started writing almost immediately.

You may be saying to yourself that it was crazy to think I could start my own bank. Maybe it was crazy, but I still pursued the idea and look what it led to! Justin helped me set up the technical side and I started writing like crazy. My articles were horrible compared to what they are now. They were full of grammar errors, run on sentences and in some cases made no sense. But people still liked them! (Yes, I know I still have some errors)

When I started my blog I had no plans to make money with it. I did not even know how blogs made money. I just assumed I would figure all that out later. If I didn't make money, I figured it would still be fun and exciting. I didn't know what affiliate marketing was or what sales funnels were or any of that. I learned as I went.

HOW WAS I ABLE TO START A SUCCESSFUL REAL ESTATE AGENT BUSINESS?

Two of the other most important decisions I ever made in my career were not planned in detail. I got into the REO business because a random company asked me to do a BPO. I researched what a BPO was, found the business of listing REOs (foreclosures), and started calling banks right away asking how I could list houses for them. Those banks put me on the right track, I did what they said to do and I started getting REO listings. Then I started going to conferences, bought REO training courses, joined REO organizations and things really took off.

I did not create a massive business plan, stress about what could go wrong or procrastinate when I decided to get into REO. I talked to a couple of people about it, realized I wanted to be in that business and I took action, even though I had no clue what I was doing.

Another huge milestone in my career was when I bought out my father's business in 2013. It all started when I asked Justin if he wanted to work for me. I knew he didn't like the corporate world and wanted a way out. I thought hard about asking him, because we were very good friends and I didn't want to ruin that. Once I decided I needed to ask him, because it could change his life for the better if I did. But I didn't have it planned out what he would do, when it would happen or how he would get paid. I assumed that would work itself out. Luckily it did and because he started working with me I was able to buy my Dad out. I didn't have a clue about payroll, employees and all of that, but Justin did, or at least he was able to figure it out.

I had thought about buying out my Dad for a long time, but I knew it would be a massive task. We had the flipping business, the real estate agent business and a couple of assistants and agents on the team. I knew I needed to take over, because I had a lot of ideas that were not being implemented. I did not know how I could afford to buy him out or how I could handle running the business. Luckily deciding to work with Justin gave me the management person I needed to figure everything out.

When I asked my father about buying him out and taking over, I did not have everything planned. I asked him if he was interested and when he said yes, we figured it all out.

HOW HAVE MY PLANS AND BUSINESSES CHANGED WITH RENTALS?

I don't have all the answers for everyone. Maybe I got lucky in by business by not planning everything out and just doing it. However, I know many people who get stuck in the planning stage and never try. I think it is definitely better to try to make it, than to not try and wonder if you could have made it. I am also a huge fan of using my time efficiently. I try to do things that bring me the biggest return on investment or are the most fun for me to do. I don't like spending hours or days on a business plan and what if nobody cares that I have a business plan?

I see a lot of people create huge, detailed business plans relating to rentals. It is great that you are writing down what you want to do and how, but does anyone else want to know? If you are trying to get private money, the investor is not going to read a giant business plan. He wants to know the numbers and your experience. A bank will want to know your financials and the properties financials. When I decided to buy rental properties I did not have a business plan. I researched the best ways to invest and I knew rental properties were the way to go. I started creating simple projections for how much money I would make after buying a certain number of properties. When I saw those numbers I got excited and knew I had to buy as many rentals as I could. Creating a detailed business plan would have frustrated me and killed my momentum.

I took way too long to buy my first rental, but I did eventually buy it in 2010. Then I bought more and more. I was using the snowball method to pay off my rentals at first, because I thought it was a good idea. After looking at the numbers, I realized paying off my rentals, was not the best use of my money. I should be reinvesting that money into more properties or using it to flip more properties. My plans changed and I made more money because of it. It is very hard to know exactly how everything will work out in business until you start and see what happens. One problem with an extremely detailed plan that you spend a ton of time on, is that you are more likely to be stuck to it when obvious changes could improve things.

CONCLUSION

Business plans are needed for some situations and some investors. For many businesses and ideas they can be a burden and keep you from taking action. If you hit a road block when trying to start a business, sometimes the best thing you can do is to take action. Forget about all the details, the what if's and just see what happens. There are many businesses that can be started without risking your livelihood or your life savings. You also do not need a brilliant idea to start a business. My silly idea to start a bank turned into Invest Four More.

29.   IS THE PURSUIT OF MONEY ALL THERE IS TO LIFE?

One of the things that makes me happiest in life, is not making money, but living life how I want to. Money can make it easier to live life how you want to, but you can't let the pursuit of money ruin the rest of your life. I think it is important that we remember money is not the ultimate goal, but a means to what we really want. We are all different as well, some people may not need much money to live their perfect life, while others may need a lot of it! To live life to the fullest, you have to be aware of how you are spending your time and maximizing the time you have. It takes a lot of effort to make sure you are living how you want to be living. It is really easy to get too busy, or forget how little time we have. When you ask really successful people what they would have done different at the end of their lives, they usually say they should have enjoyed life more, not just chased the money. That doesn't mean it is bad to chase money, it doesn't mean you can't be really happy and really rich, but I think you must focus on what that money represents, not just how much you have.

One of the biggest "aha" moments I had in life, was when I listed what I want in life regardless of what it costs. I stopped limiting what I wanted in life, based on what I thought I was capable of. I then had to figure out how I was going to achieve the things I wanted, even though I was nowhere close to making the money that was required to buy those things. Once I had the belief that I could get those things, the way I worked and saw life changed completely. My thought process about business, work and life changed. At the same time I was driven to succeed, which takes time. While I love to make money, I have to remind myself that it is not all about making money, but what money gives me. Money can give me freedom, peace of mind, a Lamborghini, health and a happy family. Money can also take away health, make your family very unhappy, and be harmful if you become obsessed with it and sacrifice too much to get it.

ARE YOU LETTING SOCIETY TELL YOU WHAT YOU WANT IN LIFE?

Before I get into how much money is enough, I want to talk about making money briefly. I believe the first step in truly being happy and living life to its fullest, is learning what you really want in life. Society and the news is full of negative talk. Whether it is politics, celebrities, world events, crime or anything from the media, it is usually bad. You would think we live in one of the most dangerous times in society with all the terrorism and mass shootings going on. We actually live in one of the safest times in the history of the world, and if you live in the US, you most likely have a pretty awesome life.

The media also loves a great story on how the rich and famous have fallen or are not nice people. It would be easy to think everyone with money is greedy, takes advantage of people and work 100 hours a week. There are studies that show money does not equal happiness, which lead many people to convince themselves being rich is bad. Although more recent studies, show that money does equal happiness and the more of it you have, the happier you are.

Being frugal is also the "in thing" right now. The less money you spend on things the better, no matter how much time it takes. There are thousands of websites about being frugal, and even some very popular sites that convince people anyone who isn't frugal is evil. My point is, if you listen to enough people and stop thinking and feeling yourself, you will mask what you really want in life. Or worse, you will justify to yourself that you should now want what you really want, because being rich is bad or will make you a bad person. Don't let anyone else tell you what you need to be happy. Figure it out for yourself and then figure out how to get it.

IS BEING FRUGAL BAD?

I want to make a very important point before moving on. Being frugal is not always a bad thing, but you can't let it rule your life. I think saving, and investing as much as you can is the best way to get ahead. But your end goal cannot be to save money until you die. You also have to decide if it is worth it to spend 8 hours going through coupons to save $15 at the store. Our time is worth money, and saving at all costs is not worth it. Saving and being frugal should get your journey started, not be the end goal.

Do not use being frugal or thinking the rich are evil, as an excuse not to chase your dreams. The biggest reason most people do not chase their dreams, is they don't think they can achieve them. That is why I stopped wanting a Lamborghini in my 20's. I didn't think I could ever have one and blocked out the dream of wanting one, because I did not want to be disappointed. That was one of the biggest mistakes I ever made. If I give up on a dream, there is no way I will achieve it. If I don't give up and I believe I can reach that dream, I might actually do it. I would much rather try to get something and fail, knowing I gave it my all, than to never try and wonder what if.

HOW MUCH MONEY IS ENOUGH?

I am not going to tell you what your dreams should be, because we are all different. Some people don't care about cars at all, some people want cars to be their life. They collect, they race, they modify, they sell, and they get involved with cars however they can. For others a passion may be art, houses, travel, writing, educating or charity. Whatever your dream is, do not block it because you are scared of failing or are worried what society will think of you. You should not limit yourself, because of what you think is realistic either. None of us know what will happen in the future, so don't assume you will never get it! How much money you need, will depend on how big your dreams are and how much they cost. Some people want to be billionaires so they can change the world.

186

There is a lot more to being successful, than simply deciding what you want in life. When you start to make money, or have made a ton of money, how do you know when to slow down and enjoy life?

First off, I do not think there is a rule that says you cannot enjoy life while making a lot of money. If you do what you love for a job, it does not feel like work. If you have a business set up correctly, you don't have to work 80 or 100 hours a week. I have multiple businesses that I run, which make me more than $100,000 a year. I talk to people all the time who tell me they never want to be me, because they do not want to work all the time. Guess what? I work about 40 hours a week. I took a ten-day vacation last month to Florida, where I did maybe 10 hours of work, which included looking at houses in the area (that was a lot of fun for me). Could I make more money faster if I worked more hours? Maybe working more would make me more money, but I also come up with some of my best ideas when I am not working. I also have 4 year-old twins and an awesome wife, who I love spending time with. If I don't spend time with them now, I will never get that time back. I have heard other entrepreneurs say, you have to focus all your time and effort on your business and you cannot have a balanced life. I don't buy that.

My kids are awesome and every year they get older and change a lot. There is no way I can ever go back in time and see them at the age they are now, or last year or the year before. It is not worth it to me, to say I can sacrifice a few more years working 80 hours a week so that my kids have a better life later on. I have no idea what the future will be like or that 80 hours a week will create a better life. My plan is to make as much time for my family and kids now.

There is still a lot I want to accomplish in life and I am by no means done growing. It is definitely possible to grow a business, make a lot of money and live a fulfilling and rewarding life. You have to set up your business correctly, be willing to hire people to help you, and not lose focus on what is important.

HOW AM I CONSTANTLY CHANGING THINGS AND SIMPLIFYING?

In the beginning, it may take 80 hours a week or more to get things set up and working right, but you have to make sure that is not your entire life. You need to have a goal for your business or investing. If you are going to work 80 hours a week, what goal do you have to reach before you change things? When will you hire help? Is your business completely depending on you working it? I worked 80 hours a week, for a short time when REO was booming. I quickly changed things by hiring an assistant, because I knew I was not happy.

I still talk to my coach from Jack Canfield Coaching, which I completed almost three years ago. In 2016 I have started to feel things were getting a little too crazy for me. I was answering a lot of email, which takes up so much time. I am doing webinars, writing books, the podcast, doing coaching calls, and being interviewed (I have been on Realor.com, Zillow, Trulia, Huffington Post, Time, Forbes and other sites recently). I feel like I was getting too scattered in my work life, and it started to affect my time for other things as well. I told my coach all of this and he said, I need to make sure I am delegating more and focusing on the things that I love to do and are the most profitable. He also said, I should be able to go on vacation for 6 months, and come back to work like nothing changed.

I am basing what I will do, based on what I love to do.

- **I love to write**. Even after three years and 400 articles, I still like to write articles. I also love writing books.
- **I love interviewing people**. I love doing the podcast interviews, because I learn as much as anyone. It is also great to network with successful people.

- **I love doing videos.** I love filming before and after videos of my flips and rentals. I like doing the videos for my coaching products, but it is not quite as much fun.
- **I love helping people.** I love creating articles and books that help people invest better or live life better. I like coaching, but that is tricky. Some students take initiative, are great to work with and listen to what I say. Others want everything done for them, refuse to listen to what I say because they know better (even though they never bought a house), get angry when I can't tell them exactly what to do, when to do it, and want me to loan them money to do it. Of course, even if I did all that, they wouldn't listen to me anyway and they would probably use the money to buy a car or something for "marketing". I have contemplated ending my coaching programs, but I can't do it because of the people who do listen and I help. Remember, just because I have coaching programs now, does not mean I will always have them. Especially when I decide to spend 6 months in Turks and Caicos (way better than the Bahamas).
- **I love to buy houses!** One of my favorite things to do is buy houses, whether they are flips or rentals. The last six months, I feel I am spending so much time on the blog, that I am not spending enough time investing.

Why am I telling you all of this? I want to show you that even though I have tried to set things up to run without a ton of work from me, things constantly change. You have to be careful that you are not taking too much on, and sacrificing your own happiness for money or success. I am simplifying things greatly in the next month or two. I don't know exactly how yet, but I cannot spend hours each day on email, I cannot take as many appointments to talk on the phone, I cannot personally post and respond to everything on Facebook, twitter, LinkedIn, YouTube, etc. Sometimes I feel I have to do it all myself, because other online real estate sites teach without ever having been in the business. Or they have coaches who haven't invested in a decade. They have people chiming in on forums, who have never bought a house, but feel they can tell people how they should invest. It is very confusing, and I wanted to provide one voice to people to provide clarity. At the same time, I know I can still provide value and help people, without doing it all myself.

WHAT IS YOUR END GOAL IN LIFE?

While I am not there, or close to it yet, I want to be able to take a 6 month vacation without working and worrying about my business. When will I get there? Who knows, but I am going to start working on it now. I also would not stop doing the things I love on vacation either, like writing a little, shooting a few videos or talking with my mastermind group. It reminds me to focus on the big picture and not worry about all the little stuff. The money is not important, what the money can give you is important. It can provide freedom, a chance to enjoy life to its fullest, healthier lifestyle and much more. When you lose focus on what you are working so hard for, it all becomes a lot less fun.

WHAT IS THE NEXT STEP?

When I work with people as a coach, my goal is to **help them make as much money as they possibly can with real estate.** Different people have different goals and like doing different things. I help some investors buy more rentals, I help other learn to flip, and I even help people become successful real estate agents. Two of the real estate agents on my team made over $100,000 in their first year! Those results won't happen for everyone, but there is a lot of money to be made in real estate.

This book lays the ground work for how to be successful in any field. I found success in real estate and that is my focus. I am a current investor and Realtor working in today's market (at least at the time of the writing of this book in 2016). If you want to get involved in real estate I would love to help you learn the ins and outs. It is not as easy as they make it look on television.

If you invest the right way, rental properties and flips can change your life. They changed my life, by giving me a better way to invest, a better way to make money, a better way to retire. I am 37 years old now and am in a better position to retire right now than most people will ever be. I am by no means done!

There is a lot going on at my blog Investfourmore.com. I have a podcast, a forum, the blog, eBooks, paperback books, coaching programs and many videos. I encourage you to sign up for my email list, if you have not already done so. The emails I send you, will help you navigate through the site, give you the most valuable resources and help you decide how much or little you want to be involved with real estate.

- You can sign up for my email list here: https://investfourmore.com/real-estate-investor-email-subscription/

- If you are interested in becoming an agent, I have a separate email list with more resources here: https://investfourmore.com/real-estate-agent-email-subscription/
- If you want to learn even more about rentals, I recently wrote Build a Rental Property Empire, a 350 + page book available as an eBook or paperback. This book is a best seller and an incredible resource. http://www.amazon.com/Build-Rental-Property-Empire-no-nonsense/dp/1530663946/ref=asap_bc?ie=UTF8
- If you want to become a real estate agent, I just came out with How to Make it Big as a Real Estate Agent, which is a 200 + page book on how I sold over 200 houses in one year and how I created my team. I am still an agent, but rarely talk with sellers or buyers, my team does it all. http://www.amazon.com/How-Make-Real-Estate-Agent/dp/153366160X/ref=asap_bc?ie=UTF8
- I have a fix and flip video training course here that has over 3 hours of video and more resources for learning how to successfully flip houses. https://shop.investfourmore.com/product/fix-and-flip-video-training-course/
- I have a quick start video training program that shows exactly how I get awesome deals. Including videos of me touring potential deals and how I search the MLS. You can find my coaching products on my blog here: https://investfourmore.com/resources/

I have made my books and coaching products as affordable as possible. I know people who are starting out in a new business, do not have a lot of extra money. For those of you who know you need a little extra push and accountability, I created more in depth training courses. These come with conference calls and email training with me personally. The Complete Blueprint for Successful Real Estate Investing is a rental property program that I created and comes with personal coaching from me as well as audio CD's/MP3s, videos, a huge how to guide and much more. If you are interested send me an email and I may have a special coupon for those that read this book all the way through! Mark@investfourmore.com.

I hope you enjoyed the book and if you want connect we me on social media check out the links below:

- Facebook
- LinkedIn
- Twitter
- Instagram
- Google +

SUGGESTED READING THAT HELPED ME LEARN THESE TECHNIQUES

- Think and Grow Rich
- Deep Work
- The Power of Now
- The War of Art
- Too Perfect
- The Kybalion
- Think Big
- Eat that Frog
- Four Hour Work Week
- The success Principles
- The Emyth
- Third Circle Theory
- Millionaire Fastlane

INSPIRATIONAL SELF-HELP LEADERS

- Jack Canfield
- Jim Rohn
- Anthony Robbins
- T Harv Ecker
- John Assaraf
- Zig Ziglar
- Darrin Hardy

ABOUT MARK FERGUSON

I created Invest Four More to help people become real estate investors either as rental property owners, flippers, wholesalers, real estate agents, and even note owners. You may see pictures of me with my Lamborghini. It is a 1999 Lamborghini Diablo, which I bought in 2014. I had dreamed of owning a Lamborghini since I was a kid, and one of my public goals I wrote about was buying one in 2014. It was an awesome experience making that goal, being held accountable by my readers, and then accomplishing it. I even make sure I buy my cars below market value. I bought this car for $126,000 and it is worth about double that two years later.

The car is not a flashy marketing ploy, but a reward for hard work and to signify that we really can have what we want, if we out our mind to it.

HOW DID I GET STARTED?

I have been a licensed Realtor since 2001. My father has been a Realtor since 1978 and I was surrounded by real estate in my youth. I remember sleeping under my dad's desk when I was three while he worked tirelessly in the office. Surprisingly, or maybe not, I never wanted anything to do with real estate. I graduated from the University of Colorado with a degree in business finance in 2001. I could not find a job that was appealing to me so I reluctantly decided to work with my father part-time in real estate. Fifteen years later I am sure glad I got into the real estate business!

Even though I had help getting started in real estate, I did not find success until I was in the business five years. I tried to follow my father's path, which did not mesh well with me. I found my own path as a REO agent and my career took off. Many people think I had a huge advantage working with my father, and he was a great help, but I think that I actually would have been more successful sooner if I had been working on my own and forced to find my own path.

Now I run a real estate team of 10, who sells 100 to 200 homes each year. I fix and flip 10-15 homes a year and I own 16 long-term rentals. I love real estate and investing because of the money you can make and the freedom running your own business brings. I also love big goals and one of those goals is my plan to purchase 100 rental properties by January 2023.

I started Invest Four More in March 2013 and the primary objective was to provide information on investing in long-term rentals. I was not a writer at any time in my life, until I started this blog. In fact I had not written anything besides a basic letter since college. Readers who have been with me from the beginning may remember how tough it was to read my first articles with all the typos and poor grammar (I know it is still not perfect!). My goal has always been to provide incredible information, not to provide perfect articles with perfect grammar.

The name "InvestFourMore" is a play on words indicating that it is possible to finance more than four properties. The blog provides articles on financing, finding, buying, rehabbing and renting rental properties. The blog also discusses mortgage pay down strategies, fix and flips, advice for real estate agents and many other real estate related topics.

I live in Greeley Colorado, which is about 50 miles North of Denver. I married my beautiful wife Jeni in 2008 and we have twins who turned five in June of 2016. Jeni was a Realtor when we met in 2005, but has since put her license on ice while she takes care of the twins. Jeni loves to sew and makes children's dresses under the label Kaiya Papaya.

Outside of work I love to travel, play golf and work/play with my cars.

ACKNOWLEDGEMENTS

I could not be where I am at without a lot of help from many people. I tried to go at it alone when I first started in the real estate business. I thought I was smart and could figure it out, without anyone else telling me how to do things. I let my ego make some very bad decisions for me. Here are a few people I have to thank.

My Dad Jim Ferguson, who has been an entrepreneur most of his life. He taught me a lot about flipping houses and being a real estate agent. He was very patient with me, when I was not patient with myself.

My wife Jeni, who has been incredibly supportive through the good times and the bad. The year I met her, I made $28,000 (2006). Things were not easy in the beginning and it was a struggle for me to break out of the grind and find my way in real estate. She was there for me when I started to find success and was working 80 or more hours a week to get everything done. She put up with me working on vacations and never really taking time off in the beginning. Luckily, I was able to create a business where we can now take real vacations without me working, where I rarely work more than 40 hours a week (if that), and we have a wonderful family. Most importantly she supported my car addiction!

Justin Gesso is my team manager and keeps our team together. He works with our agents, helps with the blog, helps with my coaching programs, helps with my books and keeps me sane. Thank you Justin!

Nikki True has been my assistant for 6 years. She was the person who helped me stop working 80 hours a week and take control of my life. She has always been extremely proactive, has an incredible work ethic, and been willing to work on any project. She is now helping me with my flipping business and doing an amazing job.

John Pfalzgraff has been our team's contract manager for many years. He is the reason I can make offers while I am still viewing a home. He keeps tabs on all the details that I hate thinking about. He is integral to our real estate agents success and mine.

Jack Canfield coaching was a program I took a few years ago. It gave me the confidence to buy my father's business, take the blog to new levels, hire more staff, and take more chances. Not only that, but I gained more freedom, reduced stress, and am a happier person because of it. My personal coach John Beaman is still someone I talk to on a monthly basis.

Josh Elledge with Upend PR has helped me be featured on numerous major media sites like Washington Post, Yahoo, Zillow, The Street, Forbes and many more.

SPECIAL BONUS AND INVESTING TOOLS

I have reached millions of people with my books and blog posts. I receive success stories all the time about how my books, articles, and coaching products have helped people.

I have many free resources on my website, an awesome podcast, and much more.

I written multiple books, created video coaching programs, and created coaching programs with personal help from me.

To learn more about what I have to offer, check out this page and get your special discount code.

https://investfourmore.com/bonus

Made in the USA
San Bernardino, CA
15 December 2016